McBeth and the Everlasting Gobstopper

Dave Fogelstrom

Rusty Weaver

ISBN: 149473334X
ISBN-13: 9781494733346
Library of Congress Control Number: 2014922383
CreateSpace Independent Publishing Platform
North Charleston, South Carolina

DEDICATION

We want to thank our families for putting up with all of our stories from the classroom, for being patient while our noses were buried in novels and plays, and for always being long suffering while our faces and thoughts were hidden behind piles of essays. Of course, we want to thank our students for giving us endless material for this book and infinite reasons to wake up in the morning and head to the classroom. We are blessed to have the greatest job in the world. To all the teachers who read this book, you have our greatest respect and admiration. It takes skill to make such a hard job look easy. Our hats are off to you! As you read this, we hope it lets you know that you are not alone in the craziness that is the classroom. Oh, and we hope it makes you laugh a lot.

ABOUT THE AUTHORS

 Rusty Weaver was educated in French at Belgian schools in the former Belgian Congo through junior high and then boarded for four years at an East Coast prep school. After graduating from college in Southern California in 1968, he taught elementary school for a year before being drafted during the Vietnam War. After five years as an aircraft navigator in the USAF, he returned to elementary school teaching. His family moved to Hawaii in 1980, where he earned a master's degree in special education. He worked briefly in that field in Hawaii's public schools before being hired as a reading, writing, and study skills specialist at a private secondary school, where he and his wife taught until their retirements. They now live in Tumwater, Washington, where they enjoy the proximity of their two children and five grandchildren.

Dave Fogelstrom grew up in the San Francisco Bay Area in the sleepy suburb of Clayton. He was active in Young Life and played football and basketball throughout high school. After graduating in 1987, he later attended Whitworth University, where he majored in English and played football. When he graduated in 1992, he came back to California and took a job at Antioch Junior High School as the drama teacher. To escape crazy eighth graders, Dave later went to Deer Valley High School in Antioch, where he taught English and coached football. In 2005, Dave transferred to Heritage High School, where he has worked up until present as a teacher, coach, and advisor to the Fellowship of Christian Athletes club. Dave lives in Brentwood with his wife, Tracy, his daughter, Hannah, and his son, Jacob. Rusty was Dave's mentor teacher for a month in college when Dave convinced his parents to send him to Hawaii for an exchange program at Kamehameha School. Seeking a month away from the cold winters of Washington, Dave found a friend and coauthor at a time when his ambition was just to get a good tan.

"Oh, what learning is!"
—*Romeo and Juliet* Act III

CHAPTERS

1

THE MOURNING BELL

Fair is foul, and foul is fair:
Hover through the fog and filthy air.
Macbeth Act I

H ave you ever been to Penis Land?
You won't find this distinctive geographic location on any
map. Please refrain from Googling it, at all costs. It exists in
the creative mind of an eighteen-year-old high school student. I cannot claim to have been to Penis Land, but a colleague of mine can.

As a government teacher, my friend assigned a project in which
students were to create their own society, complete with its own
economy, government, and geographical details. A group of boys immediately went to work on the project. When the day of their presentation arrived, they "honored" this teacher, whose last name begins
with *Pen-*, by naming their fictitious world "Pen Island." Flattered,
the teacher allowed the boys to proceed. The class enjoyed hearing
about Pen Island and its many idiosyncrasies: the phallic shape of the
map, the "seamen" who worked the docks for international trade, the
mine "shaft" where precious metals were dug up, and the flag that
flew "erect and tall" for all to see.

You see, the labyrinth of the teen mind can be difficult to traverse. The adult worldview does not immediately grasp juvenile thoughts, especially during mundane classroom presentations. Before too long, though, the teacher caught the creative pun and put the brakes on the Penis Express, and the boys headed back to their seats as high school legends. This crew might find a research paper on Canada's East Pen Island wonderful fodder to further develop the joke.

After hearing about this during a teacher therapy session in the lunchroom, I wondered if all teenagers had picked up on the joke, or just a few of the more in-tune youngsters in the room. Like my colleague, I had failed to identify the genital reference. I decided to use my daughter, a ninth grader, as a test case. How long would it take her to catch on? I told my seemingly innocent daughter about an assignment she would have to do during her senior year and detailed that one group had just done a project in honor of Mrs. Pennington in which they had christened their world "Pen Island."

Within seconds, my daughter looked at me, laughed, and then said, "Penis land. Funny." She then went back to staring at her iPhone screen. I felt older than ever.

The next morning, the local paper's headline read, "Poor Penmanship Thwarts Robbery." I slowly drank my coffee, used my index finger and thumb to clear the corners of my eyes, and tried to focus on the newspaper in front of me. Maybe it was the use of the Shakespearean-sounding *thwarts,* or perhaps it was the term *penmanship,* but I just had to read more. After the first sentence, I discovered that the age of the suspect and the location in which the bank robbery had been attempted both matched up with a school district where I had worked some years before. Could this have been a former student?

It turned out that the teller could not decipher the note that had been given to her by the potential robber, so she had asked another teller to help crack the code on the wrinkled piece of paper. More and more people in the bank became aware of something bizarre going on, and soon the alarm was pushed. The would-be thief became overwhelmed with confusion: his intricate bank-heist plan had been foiled by his poor penmanship and inability to construct a sentence. It might have been the first time that a failure of the public school system had truly benefitted society. The name of the "laughable criminal" was unfamiliar to me, but he had grown up in the city where I had once worked, so I am quite sure that his scholarly approach to writing had been molded by some of my colleagues.

Not sure whether to be happy or sad about the incident, I headed out to my car, glad that I hadn't left teaching to become a bank teller. After years of reading scribbled essays, I, without a doubt, could have read that robbery note. A bank would have lost some serious cash that day because of my unique skill set.

Such expertise goes beyond reading chicken-scratch and comes only from locking yourself in a room with pubescent children and attempting to keep their attention. The most difficult minefield for a teacher to traipse across? The products of the darling of the Elizabethan stage—the soul of the age—our friend, Mr. William Shakespeare. Just starting a unit on Shakespeare can be a daunting task for any teacher. It takes preparation, focus, and some caffeine.

As I arrived on campus at seven, I found myself standing before the soda machine. It was Shakespeare kickoff day—the day when for the first time, my students would, through the Bard's sacred words, explore the highest peaks and lowest depths of human nature. The dollar in my desk reserved for the band-fund-raiser chocolate bar would be put to better use this morning; I knew I would have to read every difficult section of the play aloud, so purchasing a caffeinated beverage was in order because we were down to just decaf again at home. I took from my pocket and slipped into the slot a perfect copy of the model displayed on the machine. George Washington looked at me with the top of his head to my left. The machine ingested the dollar but promptly spit it out.

I smoothed the bill and tried again. Failure.

I smoothed it again.

No Pepsi.

Thinking like the good, flexible teacher I still am, I got outside the box for a moment: I took George's head, turned it upside down, and shoved the wrinkled dollar into the machine. It worked. Contrary to every instruction, every logical step one should take, the converse of universally accepted and appropriately applied theory had worked, so I had my liquid motivator for the day. It took me years, though, to apply to my classroom the wisdom I had gleaned from that moment.

This sums up the reality of teaching. Everyone can tell you the proper methodologies to implement, how to use Bloom's Taxonomy (if such a thing is even studied anymore), and how to develop the multistep lesson plan according to Instructional Theory into Practice modules. However, when you follow those methods, you are usually teaching colleagues or future educators in credentialing classes. They know how to behave in class. They know they will have to get up and take your place at the front of the room soon. In this controlled environment, educators thrive in a hothouse of learning bliss.

Everything changes once you walk into a roomful of teenagers. I once stood behind a student in the nacho bar line at lunch. That seemingly mundane experience forever changed me. This young scholar's pants could have fit three of him. His football jersey hit his knees. He wore a headband, which I suppose kept the sweat off of his face as he studied furiously throughout the day, and he completed his outfit with sweatbands around his wrists to prevent his pen or pencil from slipping while composing analytical essays of the highest quality. He was also wearing batting gloves in case the sweatbands exceeded their capacity for moisture. I have no doubt that you can find these outfits sported by the scholars of Oxford and Cambridge. They are the latest rage, except that in England their sweatbands are cashmere, and a football jersey means something totally different and can get you attacked by hooligans if you wander away from the local team's fan base.

As the student began to select items for his nacho mountain, I noticed that he had loaded his plate so high with chips that adding even one more item to this caloric pile would have been a recipe for sure disaster. Totally oblivious, he next moved to the melted cheese. I kept thinking, *This kid will never make it past the sour cream.* He piled the cheese sauce until the chips were no longer visible. He then added beef, chicken, tomatoes, salsa, lettuce, shredded cheese, jalapeño peppers, and a full ladle of sour cream on the top. He had boldly and blindly defied the laws of physics, which is perhaps another reason that kids see school as a waste of time: even the law of gravity does not apply to them.

As this monstrous meal started to soak through the boy's paper plate, great drops of clumpy cheese dripped down his arm, splattering the floor as he tried to pay with a hundred-dollar bill. This was the student who would walk into my room hungering for Shakespeare? This was the young man who would learn to comprehend and value the Bard, the Soul of the Age? This was the thirsting child who, prompted into a biological coma by a blood-sugar level that would quite soon register at an alarming height along with his sodium intake, would come into class to discuss tragic figures, symbolism, and a shift from the iambic to the spondaic? I made my own salad—much smaller, of course—and paid with a pittance of coins gathered from my car's ashtray. With the morning Pepsi coursing through my veins as the only defense against the demotivating image of my nacho nightmare, I wandered up the stairs to open the door and to crack the pages of my beloved Shakespeare.

With all this in mind, I entered my classroom as the early-morning sun rose above the trash cans and parking lot lights. I always arrive early to school. Sitting in solitude in my classroom, reading through the Shakespearean scenes to be taught later that day, makes me feel I am in the presence of genius and puts me in a scholarly mood. I even throw on some Mozart now and then to spark the brainwaves, though currently, Pandora Radio is blocked due to the dearth of bandwidth in my school district. We are probably still on dial-up. Of course, in a few years, when the *Baby Mozart* DVD generation starts arriving, I might have to hand out bottles and bouncy seats before starting class. I can still get YouTube to work, though.

If I knew how to tie a bow tie, one would be part of my Shakespeare persona as well, because, unless you are a clown, wearing a bow tie somehow makes you look smart. Just look at the old school professors in black-and-white pictures, and you'll see bow ties galore. A friend told me that the world-renowned Shakespearean scholar Stephen Greenblatt wore a cape when he taught for a term at UC Berkeley. While I am not sure that is a true story, I'm quite sure I could not pull off the cape caper. But I do start the morning by having my cup of joe in a mug that has Shakespeare's face on it. That counts for something, doesn't it?

Every new teacher needs to learn the value of the early-morning arrival: it provides time each day to help students who are confused. Notify parents early in the year that you will be available in your classroom each morning to help students. When a student raises his hand right before you hand out a test and says, "I have a question. I did not get that book at all," you need only retort, "Do you really think right before a quiz is the correct time to be asking me questions about the novel? I was here this morning at seven. Where were you?"

Most drop their heads in shame, knowing full well the futility of stalling the exam with feigned confusion. No parents side with youngsters who know their teacher is sitting in a room waiting to help as the kid sleeps in or goes to Starbucks on his way to school (though some white-hat administrators do, as we'll see later when we deal with our Duncan characters).

Train yourself to get up early to open your door. Getting there before the principal arrives makes you look dedicated. Few administrators can fault you if, when they arrive on campus, your light is already on and kids are in your room. Since most teachers are idealistic in their desire to help students, there is a very real chance that God will send you a "tester student" at some point in your career. Just how dedicated are you to helping a student at the crack of dawn? Will your worldview allow someone to suck the life out of you and drain you of patience and energy? Will you help a kid despite the difficulty? Will your efforts be the dawn of a new age for some fortunate student? My own test came in the form of a young man I would soon call "the Inquisitor."

On the first day of school, this prepubescent, squinting student with a monotone voice walked into my room and introduced himself. He asked me when I'd be available to help him if he had questions. I told him, not appreciating fully what awaited me, "Every single morning, I am at my desk for any student who needs help." I also said he could come in to study in a warm, quiet place, to seek assistance with a college application essay, or just to chat. A small smile lit his face, and his eyes, less squinty than before, flickered with joy and anticipation. I sat fully cognizant that my offer would be taken up during some desperate, future point of need.

The next morning, he opened my door at 7:15 a.m. and said, "Mr. Fogelstrom, I have some questions."

Odd, I thought. *Not many people have questions before anything has actually been taught.*

The nasal-toned "Mr. Fogelstrom, I have some questions" became my morning alarm in Room C110 for the next 180 days. Nevermore did my beloved Mozart bless the morning air. My books on Shakespeare gathered dust as my morning bliss was shattered daily by the Inquisitor. Angered at first by the loss of my organizational and mental preparation time, I could not believe anyone could have enough questions to log over one thousand total minutes in my classroom before the school day formally began. Yes, I kept a calendar.

My classes were block scheduled, so the Inquisitor saw me only on alternate days for instruction, yet he arrived on cue every morning for help. Convinced that he was stalking me, I asked around, only to discover that he cornered another teacher daily during her lunch hour to ask questions until the bell rang. During his yearbook class, he would finish projects early and try to be dismissed to another teacher's room to ask questions during that teacher's prep period.

After school, he made his rounds to the few teachers penciled into his itinerary who had escaped his verbal queries earlier in the day.

The Inquisitor was relentless. During one of my few absences, a colleague told me, the Inquisitor had stood at my door with his face stuck to the window, checking to see if I might be hiding or perhaps had expired. Like a little kid looking in the candy window at desired gobstoppers, he had stood his ground for several minutes until another teacher informed him that I was out that day. The candy store was closed for the moment.

Sometimes he wanted help with grammar; sometimes it was history. Sometimes he would just say, "I don't understand what this book is about." The stunning variety of questions kept me on my toes like a boxer dodging blows. He would sit before my desk, take out his homework, and say, "I have a question." Step by step, using a methodical approach rivaled only by that of a heart surgeon, he took recordings of our discussions and penciled in answers where necessary. Only the bell and the arrival of other students for class would put a finger in the dike to cork the stream of questions, though the leak sprang afresh each new day.

Often, I crossed campus stealthily, eyes darting furtively here and there, and opened my door ever so quickly to slide inside. Before the computer powered up, before I set my backpack down, before my bottom hit my seat, my door would fly open and the Inquisitor would appear. Had he followed me to school? Had he been lurking outside in the bushes? How had I missed him crossing a campus where I had an unobstructed, clear, fifty-yard view in each direction from my door? While such questions may never be answered, here, indeed, was a candidate for the Special Forces.

By the end of the first semester, I had grown weary of the endless tutoring sessions, but on cue, the Inquisitor appeared at my door, even though he had taken my final exam the previous day. I pondered, *What could he possibly want?* I shuddered to think he desired a jump start on the second semester's material when everyone else just wanted to get to vacation.

I asked how I could help him. The Inquisitor shuffled his feet a bit and then reached into his backpack. I feared a freshly prepared list of questions related to the next ninety days of school. Perhaps he was going to video record me as I experienced another one of his interrogations. My fears quickly faded as a plate of cookies, wrapped in green-and-red paper, appeared in the Inquisitor's hands. "I baked these for you, Mr. Fogelstrom. You are a nice teacher," he said as he simply placed the gift before me. Two simple sentences. No elaboration. No frills or extras. Just two sentences, straight from the heart.

At that moment, I realized I had passed his test. Ninety straight days of tutoring in the morning and answering every question imaginable had paid off.

The cookies were delicious, though they did make me wonder who had been grilled on cookie-making directions and recipes to make this happen. His comment meant everything to me. If a teacher is really centered on students, the fact that a kid wants an hour a day, every day, should not matter. I was humbled. I thanked him, and the next semester, I greeted him with great fervor each morning when he appeared. My attitude softened, and the Inquisitor and I spent morning after morning working through his homework until his graduation day. He brought me brownies in June. He probably came by the day after school was out to ask me if I had eaten them all. I had, of course.

His picture still hangs on the wall behind my desk as a reminder to muster patience in all situations. One's reward might be watching the light click on inside a young mind, or maybe it'll just be a plate of cookies. Either one works for me.

This first chapter has truly jumped around, which I hope puts you in a bit of a confused state. If the various lines of thought befuddle your brain—good. You are now ready for high school.

2

THE INTRODUCTION

Hie thee hither,
That I may pour my spirits in thine ear;
And chastise with the valour of my tongue
All that impedes thee from the golden round...
Macbeth Act I

The introduction to *Macbeth* typically goes well. "Well" means that students sit quietly, take notes, and occasionally ask questions. The most typical question is, "Do they have a movie about this?" Today's high schoolers get their information from SparkNotes.com or the latest movie, which is why I enjoy teaching *Romeo and Juliet* and reading essays about cars, guns, and Romeo's banishment to a trailer park. Baz Luhrmann confused an entire generation of teenagers, but his film did have a cool soundtrack.

The first challenge when teaching *Macbeth* is to get students to know the correct title. Of course, immediately they think of *McDonald's* when they hear the prefix. Half of the class will spell it *McBeth* during Act I, but I get that number down to 49 percent by Act V. This means that over half of my students know by the end of our study that the usurping king of Scotland isn't a burger-joint operator with connections to the Scotland fry industry found in the Highlands, while the rest of them keep looking for a Happy Meal in the text. I should not get angry at my students though, years ago I was evaluated by an administrator during my teaching of the play. When I received my evaluation, the title was written *McBeth* in each of its appearances. Only in education would the person evaluating you and analyzing your ability to teach not be able to spell the foundational piece of your lesson. Yes, once again, irony abounds.

The next step is to explain the setting. Since senior English covers British literature, students usually have some understanding of the relationship between England and Scotland. Of course, most of this comes not from my riveting lectures and innovative teaching methods but from the movie *Braveheart*. Inevitably, someone will ask if we can watch it in class, followed by echoes such as "Hella good movie" and "Mel Gibson used to be hot, but he went crazy and got old."

The connection between the regions is invaluable because the setting comes back again and again in *Macbeth*. Like any good teacher, I assist my charges with the process of interweaving their neuron pathways with their prior knowledge. The intention is for students to file the setting into long-term memory for quick and easy retrieval. Remember the twisted and wrinkled dollar bill I had incorrectly placed in the soda machine? Its image haunts me to this day: smooth out the curriculum, insert the information correctly into the slotted instructional minutes as modeled by educational theorists, but still no soda.

After covering the historical Macbeth and Shakespeare's own sources, like *Holinshed's Chronicles*, the Gunpowder Plot of 1605, Guy Fawkes Day, and the Protestant-versus-Catholic stuff, I usually hear the observation, "I thought we weren't supposed to study religion in school? In government class, we learned about the separation of church and state."

We stop here for a discussion of what the students are doing in their government class, which constitutes what I refer to in annual objectives as my "interdisciplinary unit." Most reply, "Nothing" or in a grammatical blunder blurt out "Hella hard" when prompted to share what they have learned in class about our nation, civic pride and national politics. On my Romanticism exam each year, the most often-missed item does not concern poetic devices or poem identification but the simple matching of the American and French Revolutions with the choices "1776" and "1789," which seems to confuse half the class. The Fourth of July is just about fireworks and having a barbeque, I suppose. The year our beloved country came into existence seems lost to them.

If students establish how to spell the word *American* in their government course, a victory has been achieved. During standardized testing one year, a large number of students bubbled in "Armenian" as their nationality. They also bubbled in "graduate school" for the educational level of their parents, because, obviously, their parents had *graduated* from school. The result? When a pie chart of the school's ethnic breakdown appeared in the local papers, the shocked community became aware of a large number of Armenians on campus, many of whose parents held doctoral degrees. Unsure about the provenance of this ethnic community, people still debate the mystery.

As a result, students are no longer allowed to bubble in those sections, as a bar code is fixed to their answer documents now before they ever clutch a number two pencil or smudge a piece of scratch paper. This is a wise move by the state. I am still waiting for "Scottish" to be a choice on the ethnicity list. Anglo-Saxon is so boring and limiting.

I conclude the introduction with every senior student's favorite fact about the play: it is one of Shakespeare's shortest. That tasty morsel of information is greeted with applause and hoots of joy. I then have them read silently the section in their text that covers the background of the Globe Theater and the fast-and-loose facts about Shakespeare's life. With the riveting headings "Pomp and

Pageantry" and "Music Most Eloquent," I just don't understand why they are not hooked on the subject by the end of their silent reading.

At this point, the carrot comes into play to keep them focused: I promise to show Polanski's film version in which Macbeth gets his head cut off—if, of course, we stay on schedule. I also promise to tell them the rumors about Polanski's deviant sex life if they are really good. Without exception, this sparks students into another three or four minutes of furious reading until they hit the section in their introduction with the boldfaced heading, "The Power of Make-Believe." That always stops them cold. I have often thought of stopping here and discussing the SpongeBob SquarePants episode where he keeps saying "imagination" over and over again with a hand gesture that creates a rainbow in front of his smiling face. Worried that I might be accused of pushing a homosexual agenda, though, I prefer to let my students slowly fall asleep to the musical sounds of make-believe and stage directions.

To wrap up the period, I share with the class the "curse" of the *Macbeth* drama. I present a list of tragic occurrences that have plagued the production over the years. Some students relish the thought of attending our school production and yelling "Macbeth" at the top of their lungs when the play begins, just hoping to bring down a curse on all involved. As if high school drama teachers need screaming teenagers in the audience to remind them that their job is cursed! All most need do is look at their budgets and calculate their hourly pay rates to confirm it.

By the end of this lesson, many refuse to read *Macbeth* on the pretext that something bad will happen to them. To this I reply, "The only thing that usually gets cursed in here is your grade." This has elicited not a single laugh from a thousand-plus students over the years. You would think I would give that joke up, but some things in class are just for me, such as the time I lectured on the Enlightenment and quoted René Descartes's famous phrase, "Cogito ergo sum" (I think, therefore I am). I then announced, "According to Descartes, you have to have a rational thought to know you exist, which means many of you in here do not exist."

Nothing.

Maybe I was all alone in there.

I wish I could have talked to René.

3

CASTING CROWNS

Double, double toil and trouble;
Fire burn, and cauldron bubble.
Cool it with a baboon's blood,
Then the charm is firm and good.
Macbeth Act IV

Every English teacher dreads the challenge of assigning parts for classroom oral readings of Shakespearean plays. Without exception, the worst readers want the most complex, best-known parts.

In my first year of teaching *Romeo and Juliet*, I had a girl enthusiastically volunteer to read the part of Juliet. Without considering time constraints and her reading ability, I gave it to her and then suffered through long speeches in which she mispronounced words, incorrectly read through punctuation, stopped where no periods resided, and called up nightmares of voice inflection. It was like listening to a rap CD that skipped. The entire class slept. I tried to pull the words out of her, help her, inspire her, but in the end, all I did was frustrate the class and ruin the lesson. If a student cannot read but tries to act, at least it can be amusing; some students have no theatrical talent and read like Siri on an iPhone. I would rather have mispronounced words with a little soul behind them than correctly stated monotone lines that sound like a navigation system guiding me through each act.

It gets even worse when other students, similarly ill suited for the task, attempt to help such poor readers through difficult words. One girl was stuck on the word *yacht* in a short story. She paused before it, and I could hear the gears grinding in her head. A "nice" young man (a euphemism for a not-so-bright student) turned to her and whispered, "You pronounce that like *hatchet*, only you start it with the *Y* sound."

Two of my top students looked at me in horror, and when the girl finished the paragraph by confidently blurting out "yatchet," I made sure to pronounce *yacht* clearly and slowly when referencing events in the tale. I then said *boat* a few times to help put the word in context. Many were thinking about a yacht in the water, but some thought that a yacht (a.k.a. *yatchet*) might be a fish living in the Gulf of Mexico, though they held their questions due to peer pressure, brain fatigue, or a sugar low following the lunch bag of Sour Patch Kids and a few sodas. Had I asked them to use the word in a sentence, at least two would have written, "When I go fishing with my dad, I hope to catch a yatchet." Yes, kids, so do I.

The questions can be numbing. I had a cheery teaching methods professor in college who boldly proclaimed, "There are no dumb questions." This professor must never have heard a high school student ask, "From what part of the cow comes the chicken?" or "Our mascot is a patriot, right? So what kind of animal is a patriot?" Probably a bald eagle, kids.

By far the best and most interesting question ever heard in my class came on the heels of a video about the English language. We were watching a scene in which two men were floating in a small boat and fishing a tiny river in England. The river itself was inconsequential; the entire lesson was based on listening to the accents of the men. Of course, what the men said became of dire importance to one girl in the class.

As the men fished, one commented, "My family has been fishing this river for over four hundred years." I paused the video here to discuss the accent of the men plus the deep tradition in this village where a family has lived for four centuries. All of a sudden, one girl made a loud groan and muttered, "That's hella dumb."

Intrigued, I asked her if it was their accent that was "hella dumb" or just the fact that they had lived in this village for their entire lives as most of their family had done for centuries. She sarcastically questioned, "They have been fishing that river for over four hundred years?"

I said, "Yes, four hundred years. Grandfathers, great-grandfathers, and on and on."

She then looked at me as if she had found a secret that I, the dumb teacher, did not know. "*Four* hundred years?" she asked me again with a full eye roll.

"Yes."

"Then how are there any fish left in it?" she pointedly queried.

I sat there and held back most of the sarcastic comments I truly wanted to say, but then I decided to go ahead and unleash: "That's a great question, Cassie! How are there any fish left in it? In fact, I wonder all of the time how there are any animals in the forest, birds in the sky, or for that matter, any people still walking around after thousands of years? It is absolutely amazing. I guess it's a mystery." Obviously, our Family Life class had not prepared this young lady for reproduction beyond birth control lessons. The rest of the class just stared at her in shock. Yes, there are some dumb questions out there, and that one took the cake.

Other students have questions but don't ask them. I've had some hypothesize that double-spacing a paper means hitting the space bar twice between words. I am not kidding. I once received an essay word processed in such a manner. It must have taken hours to hit that space bar twice after each word. I should have saved it.

The questions don't cause the most disturbing moments, though. If you lack a sense of humor, watching a class of ninth graders can send you to update your résumé. You are inspired by the gods if you can explain Shakespeare to the young man I once watched blow a tiny feather, which he had plucked from the down jacket of a girl in front of him, up into the air over his nose, thereby keeping it airborne for several minutes. I was going to stop him right away, but I figured he would need a marketable skill when he got older, and the circus always has openings.

Finally, because it was distracting other students, I walked by his desk, snatched the feather out of the air, dropped it in the trash can, and continued with the lesson. He sat like a child whose candy had been stolen on Halloween night. I almost gave him the feather back out of pity. I think he plucked another from the girl's jacket in preparation for his next class period. I hope he is successful today, performing for profit under a multicolored tent.

After suffering in my early years hearing such readings and watching such behavior, I had an epiphany. No longer would I watch the class slowly die while a student struggled to pronounce the word *multitudinous*. No more would I stand by and hear my sacred Shakespeare butchered. I now cast the parts myself. Frequently, I even have a boy read Juliet's part if he is one of my best readers. This always brings a volcanic objection, to which I typically respond, "In Shakespeare's day, the actors were all male, and the female parts were played by boys whose voices had not yet changed. We can try one authentic scene in this act." Of course, the girls usually are the best readers anyway, so they need no coercion about Elizabethan tradition to nudge them on.

In that ninth-grade class, half of the boys went home after school to watch cartoons each day, while the girls had boyfriends who were seniors or were already serving in the military. Most didn't catch my puberty joke anyway. If students had actually been held back for failing a grade level, my audience, complete with beards and driver's licenses, would have understood me.

Times like these make me miss teaching eighth grade, because there I would create bizarre juxtapositions with my casting. I would call on the one male in class who was already shaving to read the part of Anne Frank. His deep voice contrasted nicely with Anne's inno-cent view of the world. At least the students understood the language of that play, though I always enjoyed the essays by kids who wrote about the Christmas gifts that Anne Frank got for Hanukkah. We teachers can't reach everyone.

An eighth grader once asserted that Arizona was the setting for Jack London's *The Call of the Wild.* Perhaps London's book shared a title with a spring break video the student had ordered with his parents' credit card from a late-night television ad. The Klondike is overrated, anyway. One of my better students claimed that the whole novel's theme came down to "do not overpack." Perhaps she was on to something. I am going to have my wife read *The Call of the Wild* this summer.

For the feather blowers of the world (and the mouth breathers), I like to add a part for a sound-effects specialist to the cast of char-acters. You never know when you'll need someone to voice Macduff's knock on Inverness's evil door.

A similar part shows up *in Romeo and Juliet* when the Nurse charac-ter is banging on Friar Laurence's cell door. Assigning a sound-effects part alleviates embarrassment for those students who fear reading aloud before their peers. Hey, and sometimes when they hit their desks to symbolize a knock, it becomes the most emotionally charged part of the period. Occasionally, I'll have one student begin to drop a nice beat, and on special days, someone else might rap, which en-ables me to bring the scene to life in a whole new way. Make one kid the wind, one the rain, one the creaking walkway, and another the drip of water from the witches' cauldron, and I have a cutting-edge learning experience for all involved.

It's amazing how students get focused on and spend massive amounts of time on irrelevant details. I worked with a science teacher who watched two of his regular grade book bottom-feeders spend an entire semester tricking out a pair of Nike shoes in the back of the room. They used pens, glue, glitter, Wite-Out, and a host of oth-er readily available items to mold a pair of sneakers into a veritable treasure. Neither of them passed the class, but both have futures in sneaker design.

Some kids will spend every minute of a class period picking out the background, font style, and color for their PowerPoint presentations if I let them. *Tell them* exactly *what you want and get them working*, is my motto. Choice can be an excellent thing, but not when the questions are "Which font is the prettiest?" or "Should each slide of a presentation have flowers, or rainbows?" or "Would red or green work best here?" or "Should my words fade slowly out or fly across the screen when I click the mouse?"

This kind of micro focus can destroy a teacher as much as it can a student. All of a sudden, one can lose perspective and end up thinking that a minuscule point is critical to a kid's future. When I taught eighth grade, we worked on making words plural. My biggest microfocus mistake was in the lesson involving dropping the *y* and adding *ies* to make the plural. It now makes me wish we still had the old Anglo-Saxon method of making words plural before the Vikings invaded England and forced everyone to add an *s*. It is important to be quite clear if you want to trade one sword for two axes though, I suppose.

The word in question that afternoon, very foreign in every way to the Anglo-Saxons and Vikings, was *jury*. I called on little Kalina to make the word plural. She blurted out, "I ain't gonna." Drawing on the single year of student teaching experience I had at that point, I went down my checklist of ways to attack this situation. First, I would reteach the concept. I strode to the chalkboard—yes, there was a time when teachers actually used chalk—and explained how to make such words plural. Then I called on Kalina again. She responded, "I don't wanna!"

This moved me to the next technique: I would salvage her self-esteem. Perhaps she was embarrassed because she did not know the answer. I cooed, "This is a safe place to make mistakes, Kalina. Let me show you on the board how we make a word like this plural. Just give it a try. I am sure there are others in here who are struggling with this concept as well." I smiled and felt great, knowing I had set things right.

She yelled out, "I don't wanna, and I ain't gonna!"

OK, so now I was running out of approaches. Reteaching had not worked. The self-esteem speech had not worked; neither had putting examples on the board. *Hmmmm*, I mused, *this must be a defiance issue.* In an authoritative voice, I said firmly and sharply, "Kalina, I have called on you, and you need to *try* to answer the question. It does not have to be correct, but you do have to try."

The class was now thoroughly engrossed in the battle to spell the word *juries*. All had dropped their pencils. I think some kids in the back were laying odds on the contest. It was the ninth inning, the bases were loaded, the game was tied, and the count was full.

Kalina blurted again, "I don't wanna!"

I was getting to the point where I presumed that she really did not want to try. It only took her assertively saying it three or four times before I finally became my father. With pointed finger, I sternly demanded, "Now, you are going to make the word *jury* plural, or I am going to send you to the office for defiance. I have stated that you are not being graded. I have shown you how to do it. I have explained this is a safe place to make mistakes. Now, I am going to ask you one last time. Tell me how to spell the plural of *jury*."

With my authority thus reasserted, I would surely hear the word *juries* spelled within the next three seconds.

"I don't wanna!"

"OK, Kalina, go to the office."

"You're picking on me!" she screamed as she walked out of the room.

I then gathered my wits and said, "OK, let's move on to number five and keep going with the lesson." I was stopped dead in my tracks, though, when a young girl in the front row raised her hand.

"Mr. Fogelstrom, aren't we going to do the word *jury*?"

I looked at her and in a moment of clear irony said, "I don't wanna."

Would Kalina ever need to use the word *juries* in a sentence? Even a felon accused of multiple crimes only has a single jury to face. I had lost sight of the world in that room the moment that making plural a word that is hardly ever used in a plural sense became the most important thing on the planet. If you find yourself ever heading down this demented path, stop, look out the window or at a picture on your desk, remember why you are there, and refocus. I threw a kid out for not trying to spell *juries*. Wow.

Someday, teachers might not need to worry about keeping their heads, because they might not even be in the room. With the Internet, kids now only need to log on to learn from virtual teachers online. Besides, kids think they know it all, anyway. They think that if they've seen the movie for a literary piece, they are up on what they need to know. In the modern film version of *Romeo and Juliet*, the one where swords are guns and horses are strange-looking cars right out of MTV's old *Pimp My Ride* program, there is a line at the end that makes no sense based on the events in the film. In the play, Prince Escalus is related by blood to Mercutio and Paris, both of whom die, but in the modern film, the police captain representing the sovereign is black, as is Mercutio, which makes sense. But Paris is the whitest guy I have ever seen. At the end of the play, Prince Escalus says:

> And I, for winking at your discords too,
> Have lost a brace of kinsmen: all are punish'd.

These lines fit with the deaths of Mercutio and Paris, but the movie also has the police captain say the line, even though Paris does not die and is white to boot, so clearly, he is unrelated to the captain. The key word is *brace*. I suppose director Baz Luhrmann figured he was making a film for teenagers who were there to see Leonardo DiCaprio strutting, Claire Danes blinking, guns firing, and gas stations exploding, so no one would be too concerned about what was actually being said.

I told my class, "Well, I guess the director figured you guys wouldn't care, and that to teenagers, a *brace* is just something for straightening teeth rather than a word meaning *a pair of something.* Maybe the police captain is seeking a dentist to fix his overbite."

A hand went up, and a girl in the second row asked, "Will we have to know that?"

"What?" I asked, puzzled.

She replied, "Do we have to know that the prince had crooked teeth?"

I smiled and retorted, "Nah, just know that somewhere in his family line there was an Anglo-Saxon."

She probably went away focused on the prince and his orthodontist, Anglo Saxon, who cannot be found in the textual notes or dramatis personae of the play but can be found in the mind of a fifteen-year-old girl who catches everything I say about as effectively as my pool sweep cleans the steps of my pool: there's stuff all over the place when the dirt and leaves settle, and it usually isn't pretty.

Sun Tzu once said, "Every battle is won before it is ever fought." Is the converse of that statement true? The first major battle in the war to teach Shakespeare begins right after parts are handed out. I ask students to turn to page 502 in the text and prepare to begin. The page number is on the board behind me, and I dutifully repeat it every thirty seconds to get them ready, yet when I sit down to read the play, only about three quarters of the students have their books open. Many are on the wrong page, some are distracted by the Renaissance pictures, and some stare blankly at the text. Others are searching for it in the grammar handbook, and the remaining quarter of the class still has its backpacks zipped tightly closed. My favorite image is the boy who is still sitting there with his backpack worn over his chest like a Baby Bjorn infant carrier. After all, that really is wonderful preparation for some of these kids.

How does a professional handle this situation? Does one yell, scream, and go into a lecture about the eternal value of being on the correct page so one absorbs the truths of Shakespeare? As I think about such moments, I reflect upon my unique approach. I calmly quiet the class by staring intently at one individual. The students eventually stop talking, probably wondering what's wrong with me. This focuses them. I used to count down from three to one, but younger students saw this as a countdown to madness or lift-off. As ninth graders are from another planet, the staring trick works best with them. Like curious dogs cocking their heads to one side in the presence of a new stimulus, the masses crink their necks, close their mouths, and wonder what is wrong with their teacher as I intently stare at the most talkative kid in the room.

Teachers must be visionary before making bold statements about standards or consequences. In any case, avoid counting down whenever possible. If you hit zero and madness still prevails, a consequence must come next, which usually means even more work, such as a referral or phone call home. Furthermore, this deadly chain of events leads to rationalizations in the vice-principal's office about why no bad behavior in the classroom is the fault of any given student.

By far the greatest ironclad "I will not budge" standard for most teachers is the dreaded due date and "no late papers" rule. I had a football player one year who failed to get his essay turned in on time. He told me, "The printer at my house ran out of ink," which most printers seem scheduled to do when major papers are due, so I told him to bring me a confirmation note from his parents, and I would consider taking the paper the next day. He asked if he could finish his project in the library and maybe get it to me that day. "Of course," I said. The library is always a great option to finish and print work, but I would still require a letter about the printer ink.

That afternoon, which also happened to be Halloween, I saw him before football practice and he started to walk out of the locker room without his pads on. I asked him where he thought he was going, since he had football practice. He said he thought I had excused him from practice to finish his paper. When I told him that I expected him to finish the paper at home or in the library at lunch, after football, or in the morning, he angrily said, "Well, I guess I can't go trick-or-treating tonight!" Silly me. How could I expect a teenager to do homework or go to football practice when Skittles and Halloween joy were so near at hand?

That is a mind-set I can't understand. It has to be hereditary. One year, we had a ninth-grade football player actually hide behind the manager's equipment buggy during sprints. He eluded our watchful eyes for at least five hundred yards' worth of sprints. Suddenly, one of our coaches yelled, "You have got to be kidding me!" and the kid sheepishly walked out from behind the blocking pads and drill cones to face the music with his teammates. He clearly did not want to run. He made it just long enough to get his face in the team picture and yearbook; shortly after, he quit. I had to admire this young man: he had a goal. He did have the best accessories on for the team picture—sweatbands, gloves, bicep bands, plus the nicest Nike ID cleats with his name embedded, so obviously he had been planning his attire for months, as well as his escape from sprints.

A few weeks later in a parent conference, after his Houdini-like escape from conditioning, I heard his dad yell, "This is exactly what is going on at home! You never do your chores. The trash cans are never put out on time. The damn dog would be dead if I didn't check to see if you fed him each night!" At least the kid was consistent. He probably didn't feed the dog because he already had great pictures posted on Twitter of the two of them together: goal achieved. It was time for him to move on to his next great escape.

When one is a senior, unfortunately, there is no place to hide, and escaping the state-mandated number of credits cannot happen, not even for the sprint avoider I encountered. If the kids are not getting their work done, all you have to say is, "Do you want to graduate?" to refocus them. The light at the end of the tunnel is much brighter for your twelfth grader. Ninth graders aren't even conscious that they are on a path to anywhere other than lunch. Getting to the proper page, though, remains a battle at all grade levels.

At this juncture, I announce, "I would like to personally invite those of you who still have your books in your backpacks to come and join us on page five-oh-two in the anthology."

This statement is traditionally followed by, "What page?"

A finger gesture toward the whiteboard where it is written in three foot high numbers usually solves the problem. We are now ready to roll and are but a syllable away from eternal truths about power and ambition, plus some nifty iambic pentameter when I bring a Shakespearean sonnet into a lesson.

The first great distraction hits my room on cue, just as Shakespeare's words are forming on my lips: office pass. An office TA enters with a sheaf of bright-yellow passes. Many students covet such passes the way Charlie Bucket did the golden tickets Willy Wonka sent out. This means an escape: out the door, time sitting in the office not having to improve one's mind, an opportunity to enjoy one's iPhone or check Twitter and text messages. Frequently, after I look at the name on the pass, I observe, "He's not here today…or on most any day." This signals the TA to leave the room without the appointed victim and with all students present that day still accounted for in their seats, which generates a chorus of groans. No one is going to see the Oompa-Loompas today. The optimist in each of them figures that, though none of them received the golden ticket and were not called out to the office, there could be a fire drill and another chance to escape. I am convinced that my former Houdini football player has pulled the fire alarm at least once. It fits his profile too well.

While scanning to see that all are prepared to discover the wonders of Shakespeare's insights into human nature, politics, and vocabulary, I frequently spot at least one student with a book open, usually a male with his hands moving under his desk. I then announce, "If any of you have cell phones or pagers, laptops or recorders, MP3 players, iPods, iPhones, iPads, iPad2s, Amazon Kindles, or a beta version of the iWatch, please power down now before I am forced to take it. If I see one, it is mine." Girls typically put phone in purse, position the purse on lap, and pretend they are looking for something essential while they text message like crazy.

Kids have more gadgets these days than James Bond's Aston Martin. I had one student who was a legend among his peers because he had created a remote-control device at home that would turn his eighth grade teacher's television on and off. He would occasionally bring it to school and click it during class. The television's volume would explode to 120 decibels and scare the hell out of the teacher. The student was wise enough to do it only occasionally so the joke kept running all year.

At one point, that kid was failing my class, so I called his father. His dad threatened to inventory and then sell on eBay every electronic device in the kid's room if he did not raise his grade. He actually sent me the list and told me to read it to the kid. Magically, the grade rose within a few days. The young man was probably preparing to launch the space shuttle Challenger from his room, so he could not afford to lose any of his sacred toys. He most certainly works for the CIA now.

Happily, the miracle cure of the parental threat is still alive and well. After my announcement about electronic devices, I always walk to the board, turn my back to the class, and take a minute to write some irrelevant comment under the homework or agenda section. This provides the opportunity for students to hide their gadgets. They probably think, "Man, is this guy stupid! He never saw my phone." This saves me from writing a referral, making a phone call home, and attending a conference with an angry parent who will explain to me why I have no right to take a cell phone from his or her child. The few times I have confiscated a phone, the last text message on the screen was from "Mom" or "Dad," which is disheartening, but not surprising.

A fellow English teacher and friend of mine was once accused by a parent of becoming a teacher just for the money and the power. I guess a firefighter becomes a firefighter just for the free water and cool hat. Money and power, indeed! While the abuse of those two nouns may be a fertile field for dramatists, the two do not connect with anything remotely related to the teaching profession.

The one thing a teacher does have in abundance is diversity in the classroom and a massive trove of strange, tragic, and comedic experiences. One rumor has it that Shakespeare spent time as a schoolmaster in England before taking up his career in the theater. After a week in a high school room, anyone could see how the profession lends itself to both comedy and tragedy.

The parts in *Macbeth* are as varied as the thirty-plus students in my classroom, but a good dramatist knows how to write dialogue for each of them. Shakespeare's incredible range and linguistic ability, from regal to rogue, remains a marvel to all who study his works. Still, as a teacher in the public schools surrounded by the panoply of society, I have an understanding of how he did it. The theory goes that Shakespeare spent time writing in taverns. In fact, some of his most diverting scenes are set in taverns. Within a tavern, a meal, a beverage, and an endless supply of light came with the pennies paid. Candles were expensive during the sixteenth and seventeenth centuries, so many found an Elizabethan bargain at the local watering hole. Comcast and AT&T cannot claim to be the first to bundle various consumer services. England's inns beat them to it four hundred years ago.

The tavern numbered personages in various states of intellect, physical condition, and sobriety. Just listening to the lawyers, sailors, vagabonds, thieves, artists, prostitutes, and others present would have provided good William with a steady supply of idiomatic expressions and linguistic specificity related to the patrons' locales and vocations. If he were writing today and sought diversity of tongue, all Shakespeare would need would be a brief stint in the school system.

In one short class period, I read and heard such assorted anecdotes that one would think I had sat next to William with a flickering candle before me, a dagger in my belt, and a dark brew foaming over the edges of its pewter cup. An innocent young girl spoke excitedly about a movie whose premiere she was anticipating due to the cute boy playing the lead, yet just over her horizon, I got the scent of a criminal, drug-related activity that weekend. I felt like I should report something to someone, but no names had been mentioned. Like Seacole, a member of the watch in *Much Ado about Nothing*, I attempted to listen and interpret the story lines being laid out, but, also like good master Seacole, I remained confused.

The ignorant members of the watch in *Much Ado about Nothing* have nothing on today's teens in terms of the misuse of language. Dogberry and Verges probably would write *collage* instead of *college* and *defiantly* instead of *definitely* on their school of choice's application. One student's personal college application essay read, "A big challenge I went through was when members of my team decided to fornicate our ideas in the video production class." I dearly hope they had not filmed those ideas, but I did hear such "fornicating" details coming from a crooked-eyed teen semiworking in the left corner of my room during cooperative learning groups. His audience was riveted to his every word. I witnessed, perhaps, a budding young Shakespeare plying his trade while delivering the salacious fine points with appropriate pauses and inflections.

Meanwhile, college-bound youngsters discussed Chaucer's satiric view of the Catholic Church. Terms such as *hyperbole* and *irony* could be heard over criminal, pornographic, and cinematic-related sidebars. This mishmash of humanity ends up as a blessing when I assign parts for *Macbeth*. Shakespeare, once again proving his profound genius, seems to know a little bit about everyone and everything, just like any good teacher. Teachers teach the high, the low, and the kids in between. Shakespeare paralleled teachers with his use of lofty language and elegant themes for the aristocracy in the audience and sex jokes and puns for the groundlings. Whether handing out parts or just watching a play, there is room for all in the Shakespeare Inn. However, some people fit certain parts better than others.

This brings us to the witches.

4

THE WEIRD SISTERS

What are these,
So wither'd and so wild in their attire,
That look not like th' inhabitants o' the earth,
And yet are on't?
Macbeth Act I

In Shakespeare's era, every dramatist faced a challenge at the outset of a performance: what to do about "the pit"—that ill-clad, malodorous rabble standing around the stage in the penny-admission area. For these proles, life was a seamless sequence of eat, sleep, work (repeat ad infinitum) and whatever entertainment they could pilfer along the way. If a penny could get one in, it also provided the opportunity to rain abuse on the performers, not just with words, but with overripe vegetables, too. Most people have only seen such behavior in cartoons, but the pelting of actors with expired foodstuffs is a long tradition rooted in the Elizabethan era.

Remember, these were the days when only the lowest of the low earned their gruel by performing for others, a time when playacting was considered slothful and sinful according to King James's Roman Catholic orthodoxy. Recall, too, that most "plays" were street skits that majored in slapstick, scandalous language, and minimal scenery. Serious drama was strictly for the ruling classes, often depicting recognizable aristocrats. Thus, a wise dramatist opened with a scene that might divert the pit, thereby allowing the drama's plot to bloom and move forward. Shakespeare was a master of this diversionary tactic. Recall, for example, the opening scene of *Romeo and Juliet*, in which Sampson and Gregory exchange insults filled with sexual innuendo—"My naked weapon is out," and all that.

American audiences relate well to the crowd in the pit, and directors realize the importance of grabbing the groundlings who have short attention spans before their minds wander far afield to conceive acts of mischief or violence stoked by boredom. Decades ago, films such as *My Fair Lady* began with long minutes of music, credits, and pictures of flowers, all before a word was spoken. Today's students scream, "Hit fast-forward!" if they even sniff a film's beginning will stall with credits.

Contemporary directors believe in starting fast. One has to wait until the film is over to find out who was in charge of casting or sewing buttons on costumes. Note that each James Bond production begins with the same tactic Shakespeare used: hit the audience hard with sex and violence, which always sell.

In *Macbeth*, the Bard employed special effects instead of sexual innuendo. The opening curtain rises to reveal a surreal setting of wind, lightning, thunder, and rain, and then spotlights a trio of gap-toothed, fully bearded harpies swirling about as they call out obscure prophecies. This was an easy scene for me to cast. In the course of my nearly forty years of teaching, I encountered at least a score of budding-witches who could have auditioned convincingly to play one of the Weird Sisters, even at the Stratford-on-Avon pinnacle of Shakespearean theater.

First Witch

Witch One appeared at my sophomore homeroom door early one September morning with two male colleagues from a speech classroom down the hall. The trio were there to solicit new members for the Speech Club and were not my own students. I ceded the dais, and they introduced themselves and their oratorical extracurricular provenance as I retired to my desk in the rear of the room. Then the cool-as-a-cucumber young lady turned to the whiteboard, took a blue Expo marker, and printed in large letters:

T.I.T.S.

There was a collective intake of breath from my homeroom and then sporadic giggles. "Wow," I thought, "what a brilliant attention-getter! Definitely worthy of Shakespeare himself. What a great coach this Speech Club has!" All eyes and ears were tuned to the speaker from then on. The groundlings were focused, and the "play" began.

Unfortunately, this thrilling and most promising opening soon lost its gusto for my students. It turned out that the acronym merely stood for Thanksgiving Invitational Tournament in Speech, which disappointed most of the boys mightily. When the young lady finished her presentation, I asked her if this meant that a four-year Speech Club student might have been to four "tee-eye-tees." My homeroom hooted gamely at my cleverness, and the hucksters moved their bit on to their next audience.

Later that day, I was summoned urgently to the male vice-principal's office, where I was informed that the young lady had complained that I had harassed her sexually and that she would be counseled by a male member of what I had come to call "the Misguidance Department."

Uh-oh! Her claim that she had intended no sexual innuendo by the acronym printed on the whiteboard had been accepted at face value, and even the Speech Department, for whom the event had been an annual highlight for at least a decade, disavowed ever having noticed the acronym's potential interpretation. I found this an interesting commentary on the Speech Department, as every member of my homeroom had instantly picked up on the allusion. Had

I left her carnal acronym on my board and continued to trumpet the praises of the Speech Department, I most certainly think I could have tripled their sign-ups the next semester. If the Thanksgiving Invitational Tournament were to have been held at East Pen Island, I think I could have retired right there with enough bawdy word play to fill a full scene of Shakespeare's first act. Sadly, the Canadian island was not the destination that year.

Second Witch

If First Witch was naïve and defensive, Second Witch was nasty from the get-go. She was big, strong, domineering, and whiny. She exacted subservience from her female classmates. She ran the sophomore class social scene like a female godfather. As the girlfriend of the superintendent's son, she had an inside line on school scuttlebutt and direct access at any time to the high and mighty. She was also venomous when crossed, as I found out repeatedly.

One day I stopped her in a hallway because she was wearing flip-flops, which were prohibited by the dress code. She growled that she'd already been sent to her locker to change them. When I spotted her a couple of hours later, still in the flip-flops, I escorted her personally to her locker to make sure she complied.

The next day, the principal sought me out during my prep period to ask why I had harassed Witch Two about her shoes. Witch Two had used her inside track to report my supposed peccadillo. Now, I don't fault teenagers for trying to blame others for their problems; it's par for the course. I do fault adults who abet them.

I incurred the wrath of Witch Two again one day when, after several warnings, I tossed her out of class for repeatedly interrupting and derailing a class discussion with argumentative and irrelevant comments. Outside the classroom door, I told her I'd be discussing the situation with the principal.

I guess it should have been no surprise when I found that she had beat me to the punch by coercing a handful of female serfs to accompany her as they cut their next class to visit the grade-level counselor to complain about a variety of claimed offenses on my part. Of course, this was before I'd had my opportunity to e-mail or meet with the principal.

Again I was put on the defensive by the witless principal before I knew anything about this. When I visited the grade-level counselor later, she swore she had dismissed Witch Two's delegation's complaints as same-old, same-old from a familiar source. This meant that Witch Two and her cronies, like children who go to Daddy when Mommy doesn't give the answer they want, had gone from the unimpressed counselor to seek a "there, there" from the principal.

The final straw with Witch Two came just prior to exams at the end of the year. I had assigned a final essay in my English classes in place of an exam, as was my option. Due to a citywide power outage, though, school was cancelled for a day between the assignment and the due date. At the request of many students, I extended the deadline for the essay accordingly, which put it off from a Friday to a Monday; it was thus due on the first day of exams, providing an entire weekend of extra time.

Without preamble of any kind, I was summoned one morning to the principal's office during my prep period and was confronted with the accusation that I had made a last-minute change to the due date of my essay such that it interfered with my students' time to study for their exams.

I was flummoxed! I had extended the deadline, which I had thought of as merciful, though nothing prevented a student from completing my final essay before the due date. Now I was being accused of interfering with study for exams in other subjects. Again the tail was wagging the dog as the principal blindly took Witch Two's claims at face value. As they say, "Fact is stranger than fiction."

Third Witch

The Third Witch haunted my life but a short while. She was a principal who took over a well-functioning school with a large minority population. This woman arrived from a lily-white environment in the Midwest with absolutely no idea what she was doing. To show her "connection" with African American students, she put a poster up in her office of shirtless basketball players on a playground. With that stereotype on board, she firmly shoved us all off into the deep waters of dysfunction.

When Macbeth takes charge of Scotland, he soon launches a spy campaign to discover any traitors in his midst. MacDuff's family falls prey to Macbeth's wrath because of rumors and suspicion provided by a paid servant. My Third Witch immediately went to work on new, unsuspecting teachers. She would invite them to lunch and then grill them ever so cunningly to reveal lunchroom conversations about administrative policies and, quite frankly, to get information about what people thought of her. Soon, after discovering that the principal had informants in each lunchroom, teachers headed to individual classrooms to eat. It felt very much like Macbeth's Scotland. We discovered that one by one, she was calling people in to find out if they were one of "her people" or the former principal's. Most amusingly, she did not understand at all the tenure system that allows teachers to keep their jobs even if the principal does not like them. She threatened to get rid of people, to transfer them elsewhere, and, all in all, it soon became a big joke if you received an e-mail from her to visit her office.

On her desk, she had one of those tiny, anti-stress Zen sandboxes complete with a miniscule rake. One teacher started to play with the rake in the middle of an interrogation, probably just to annoy her. She launched into another tirade, and he just stood up and left. Maybe a stress ball or a wind chime would have been more effective in calming her down.

In an administrative meeting, according to known sources, she reached into her jacket to pull something out and ended up with her underwear in her hand. That, of course, made all the vice-principals realize that they had an insane monarch trying to run the show. Her performance had left them feeling similarly to Scotland's thanes in the banquet scene after Macbeth's manic tirade about the nonexistent ghost.

Like Scotland under Macbeth, our school needed a deliverer. Well, this Third Witch lasted just two years before the community and district office came to understand what we all knew: there was an evil presence in the tower. I did learn a few things. Those Zen gardens that are supposed to help lower stress levels definitely do not work on witches. Or, perchance, instead of a tiny box and small, fork-sized rake, she needed an entire sandpit the size of a football field with a pitchfork pulled by a John Deere tractor. I guess the pitchfork would have been symbolic of her nature.

If Shakespeare could have taken all three of my witches and put them together as *Macbeth* opened, the play's first lines would have permeated the cursed air with such evil that the suffocated audience would have perished on the spot. The infamous curse that haunts this tragic play would have garnered another set of victims, adding to the lore of its malevolence.

And such "weird sisters" inhabit every school, as well as many "weird brothers," but that's another tale for sure.

5

THE READING BEGINS...
THE EXPLAINING NEVER ENDS

I dare not speak much further;
But cruel are the times, when we are traitors
And do not know ourselves, when we hold rumour
From what we fear, yet know not what we fear,
But float upon a wild and violent sea
Each way and move.
Macbeth Act IV

The opening of *Macbeth* has the three "Weird Sisters" chanting in unison. When you have it read orally, you can tell how the classroom readings will go within the first thirty seconds. If your three witches chant in unison, you have a great class. If only two of them are together, it will be a decent class. If they begin chanting and then fade off, stop, or just are unintelligible, you are in for a long haul. If they can't pronounce *fair* and *foul*, you should go straight to a DVD or pick up a class set of Monarch notes.

Audiobooks can also be a nice option but will bore you out of your mind. You can even find a condensed version of *Macbeth* on the Internet that will put the entire play into standard English. My industrious students find it every year, and then base their class answers on it.

In Act I, Macbeth is introduced by a bloody soldier's description. The preeminent line describes Macbeth gutting a rebel: "Till he unseamed him from the nave to th' chops, and fixed his head upon the battlements." The usual struggle here begins with the concept of being "unseamed" on a battlefield. I pose to the class, "What does this line tell us about the character of Macbeth?"

"He stole someone's clothes!"

"He's a doctor."

The "doctor" theory puzzled me until one student explained, "It says right there, Mr. Fogelstrom—he fixed some guy's head." I suppose Macbeth might have been a certified Scottish psychologist. As the Elizabethan language is baffling for students, I explain that Macbeth gutted the rebel much as one cleans a fish or a deer. Lamentably, this analogy is completely lost in that I teach in an urban environment where fish is bought at Costco and where a deer is a plastic decoration to adorn the front yard during the Christmas season. The students still confused, we move deeper into the play.

I step back and take a deep breath before attempting to explain Macbeth's various titles. In the beginning, Macbeth is "Thane of Glamis" until he receives the title "Thane of Cawdor" and ultimately, "King of Scotland." The witches predict this in Act I, which brings up the fate-versus-free-will motif that runs throughout the senior-year curriculum. I ask students, "Do you believe in destiny, or do you make your own choices throughout life?" They almost always answer yes.

Here, every single year, I reply, "Your 'yes' answer to what seem to be two mutually exclusive choices shows a deep and profound understanding of a mystical and theological debate that has raged for centuries and can be seen in the world's most famous epics. You apparently see the two ideas, *fate* and *free will*, as intertwined and cooperative. I applaud your ability to see what many have missed throughout the ages. You see a man in the bottom of a well with two ropes hanging before him. Each rope has a different label on it. One says *fate* and the other says *free will*. The man wants out of the well but cannot see more than several inches above his head."

Here, I go to the board and draw a stick figure, complete with a smiley face, stuck in a well with two ropes hanging above him. I continue, "The man grabs the rope labeled *fate* and the other rope disappears, but the fate rope does not help him out of the well. He grabs the rope dubbed *free will*, but the other disappears, and he still cannot get out of the well. Neither rope by itself is taut enough to be climbed. In a brilliant and well-thought-out move, he grabs both ropes and pulls himself out. As he comes into the light and out of the well, he sees that the rope is on a pulley and is really one rope that wraps around a wheel at the top. What looked like two choices from his limited perspective deep in the well was actually a single option. They are two ends of the same rope. So, you see, your 'yes' answer is absolutely profound in many philosophers' eyes."

This grabs them for about thirty seconds until someone says, "What is Macbeth doing in a well?"

I feel like responding sarcastically, "You see, kids, he's hiding because he took someone's clothes on the battlefield, remember?" I could even bring in Plato's allegory of the cave and his ideal forms here, but most would only envision the colored, gooey material that they used to play with when they were kids, not the famous Greek thinker.

One of the key points in Act I is that the extant Thane of Cawdor is a traitor, and that Macbeth earns that title as a promotion for leading the destruction of the rebels who sided with the King of Norway. This foreshadows Macbeth's traitorous actions in that he now owns the title previously held by a man who betrayed King Duncan. King Duncan, having been deceived by the original Thane of Cawdor, says a line absolutely critical to understanding the play:

There's no art
To find the mind's construction in the face:
He was a gentleman on whom I built
An absolute trust.

As their teacher, I want to show students the genius of Shakespeare's language. Unless one is a master poker player, it is difficult to discern from people's facial expressions what they are thinking. The point to ponder is obviously, "What does Duncan mean here about the way we see other people?" Students have strong opinions that they are eager to blurt out.

"Something is being built!"

"He can't paint!"

"He's getting smarter!"

This reveals that confusion abounds. Duncan's *art* and *construction* cannot be read beyond the literal building or painting that students do in elementary school. Maybe I should talk about Play-Doh right here. I used to like the green.

Now, a quick review is in order to boost student self-esteem, so it is time for the obvious-question technique to ignite student voices. "Students, this is difficult stuff. It gets into the deepest realms of the human psyche, so let's back up and review. Where does the story take place?"

Hands go up, with England or Ireland the most popular incorrect choices. "Good attempts, gang. You are close. Think back to a country we looked at earlier this semester when studying Edward I."

Blank stares.

"Remember *Braveheart?*"

The class perks up.

"Are we gonna watch it?"

I have already addressed this question, so I move on. "Do you know the setting for Macbeth?"

One student inevitably will go way back in time and answer, "Roman?"

I then try to explain that *Roman i*s not a country, but a word for people who lived in Rome or a description of things related to that society. This is the perfect opportunity to explain the difference between a noun and an adjective. It's what college professors of education call a teachable moment. We are truly on the razor's edge of learning now.

"I'm glad you brought this up. What is a noun?"

A hand rises. "I thought we were going to watch *Braveheart!*"

Ah, here is the chance to connect with students and use their own comments as a springboard to learning. "OK, is *Braveheart* a noun or an adjective?"

Another hand and a voice with enthusiasm: "What are those things called that those guys wore in *Braveheart?*"

Another responds, "Kelps!"

I check my pulse for a moment and then rein in the cherubs. "OK, look. To answer the most recent question: the Scottish men wore kilts, not kelps, and we are not going to watch the Mel Gibson movie. A noun is a person, place, thing, or idea, and an adjective modifies a noun. Furthermore, *Braveheart* is a proper noun because it is the name of a movie. Plus, you could call it a compound noun because it is made up of two words. So, can anyone tell me where Macbeth takes place?"

Scanning the room, I notice that some books are now closed. Time to call on Mr. Fogelstrom to answer my own question. At least I will be right. "The play takes place in Scotland, guys, so let's reopen our books now that we've discussed nouns, adjectives, and historical fiction movies and continue to the end of Act I." The choral groans emerge, books reopen slowly, and the train limps out of the station again.

Thankfully, the play is moving toward Lady Macbeth's big entrance. Here, you have to be careful in choosing a student to read her part. I prefer to read this section aloud myself because *A*, students can't read this section in under ten minutes, and *B*, I don't want them to have to say *breasts* or *unsex* aloud during certain class periods. Any word even remotely related to sex or certain human body parts can cause an immediate flare-up in class, especially at the ninth-grade level.

When I was teaching junior high, once a year I would switch for a day with the science teacher, and we would teach each other's class. He would teach an English lesson, and I would instruct the youngsters in a lab or experiment. I always left him with the section on splitting the spoils of war in the condensed version of *The Iliad* in the eighth-grade anthology. Why? So he could experience the line, "I will have no part in another man's booty" as read by a thirteen-year-old. After our first switch period, he just looked at me and shook his head as we crossed paths in the hallway on the way back to our own rooms. Proud of my practical joke, I smiled, knowing I had bested him.

The next year, though, he got his revenge when, on my day with them, his science students had to make models of the male sex organ out of tinfoil for the unit on reproduction. We were even.

The third year, my colleague was fully prepared for *The Iliad* and had even begun to embrace the "booty" line with his own comedic comments. He told me I would be showing a simple film for his science class. I figured our merry war had ended. How could a film possibly provide an awkward moment for me?

The video began. It was about cells and the immune system. As bored as his students, I sat there wondering why he would ever leave this for our yearly class switch. Students were falling asleep. Soon, though, I fell prey to his devious plan. After droning on about the immune system, the narrator suddenly brought up bacteria and infection-fighting phagocytes. While I have heard different pronunciations of this cell term, this film's narrator hit hard on the first few letters, and it sounded exactly like FAG-ocytes.

The class went nuts. Girls giggled. Boys cracked up. The beast was fully awake now. For the next five minutes, the term flew around the room like piñata candy while the film described phagocytes as "massive" and "blood filled" and detailed how macrophages are just giant phagocytes that have eaten until they burst.

I thought, *Dear Lord, please make this stop.* I had completely lost control of the class. Providence provided relief as the T and B cells entered the movie next.

I waved a final good-bye to the phagocytes and to my yearly class switch. I vowed never again to teach science. My friend had soundly defeated me. No line from *The Iliad* matches tinfoil penises or eighth graders hearing about "massive, blood-filled phagocytes" two dozen times in five minutes.

Any mention of sex or sexuality reliably wakes students up. When Lady Macbeth begins her speech about Macbeth's inability to follow through on an evil action such as murdering King Duncan, students begin to nod off. However, when she learns that Duncan is to spend the night at Inverness, their castle, she spouts words that every high school boy loves to hear: "Come, you spirits that tend on mortal thoughts, unsex me here..."

To confirm that the students understand this evil prayer, I ask, "What is she asking for here?"

Hands fly up throughout the room. "She wants to have sex with the evil spirits!" some will assert.

The important thing here is to read for context clues that might help. "I see the term *unsex* is throwing you off. Let's keep reading, because I think it will become clear to you what she is asking for," I add hopefully.

Before I've gone much further, the future lawyers intone confidently, "See, I told you she wanted to have sex! It says so right there. She wants to have sex with violent, blind priests!"

I then have to ponder in a new light the lines:

Come to my woman's breasts,
And take my milk for gall, you murd'ring ministers,
Wherever in your sightless substances
You wait on nature's mischief.

At this juncture, I fear we will never make it to the end of the play. "OK, gang, to begin with, when she says, 'Unsex me,' she is referring to the removal of traits traditionally attributed to women—traits such as compassion and the ability to nurture offspring. She is preparing herself for murder and evil. The whole conversation about her breasts is important because she is poisoning the traditional function of sustaining life through breastfeeding a child by converting milk to a bitter substance. Do you understand?"

Puzzled looks.

A hand rises. "She wants to poison her kid?"

I reply, "She does not have any children."

Another hand. "Is that because she is messing around with a blind priest?"

A deep breath and a look to the heavens to gain my composure help save the day. "There is no blind priest who is having an affair with Lady Macbeth. Lady Macbeth does not have a child whom she is going to poison with gall from her breasts. The 'murd'ring ministers' are the evil spirits, and the section that says 'sightless substances' refers to invisible beings that will assist her in the evil plot to get her husband to kill Duncan."

At this juncture, I have them reread the scene quietly to themselves while looking for the highway signs we have just discussed. This break provides a fleeting moment when I can sit, look at my own kids' photos on the wall, and remember why I do this each day.

I have one picture in particular that I look at. It is a picture of my three-year-old son at the beach. He has the biggest smile on his face that I have ever seen. The reason? He has just smashed his five-year-old sister's sandcastle to smithereens. Behind me that day, while the picture was being taken, my daughter wept for at least ten minutes, her face crusted with sand from "the battle at the sandcastle." She looked like a leaky crumb donut. Fortunately for her, she is not in the picture. This picture reminds me that tragic events and frustration can birth great joy and euphoria.

I love Shakespeare. My metaphoric castle is smashed at this point in the play because of the butchering of words, plot, and themes, but perhaps I can find joy in its destruction. One must put the pain behind and trudge on. As the saying goes, "The task of destruction is infinitely simpler than the task of construction."

At the close of the first act, Macbeth carries on an internal debate about whether or not to kill King Duncan. He creates a pro-and-con chart for himself in a powerful soliloquy. The key point for students to appreciate is that there are more reasons not to kill the king than to commit the murder. Macbeth says: "We still have judgment here; that we but teach bloody instructions, which being taught, return to plague th' inventor."

I want students to see that the old cliché is true: live by the sword, die by the sword. At the end of a gangster movie, or one that involves the rise of a drug kingpin, one never sees an old man attended by his extended family as they sing Christmas carols. The sword road just doesn't end in a nice destination. Here is where I refocus things. "OK, this is key here. Macbeth has some weighty reasons not to kill the king. What is he getting at in this speech?"

I had one student answer, "He doesn't want to kill him because he will get sick and his plans won't work because people can't read or understand his instructions."

You see, "bloody instructions," to a teenager, just means a piece of paper covered in blood or, at the very least, red ink. What's more, if something is going to come back and "plague" the inventor, this obviously means it literally will have to do with illness, disease, or catching a virus. To summarize this teen's analysis: Macbeth should not kill the king because people around him are illiterate and he could catch a virus. Beautiful.

Of course, here I move into questions about the Black Death. Queries such as, "How did you catch it?" and "What did the people look like when they were dying?" fill the air. Clearly, students want to know if it was "hella gross" and if it could happen again.

One year, this turned into a full-fledged mini seminar about how germs spread. The class cringed as words such as "vomit" and "rash" were thrown about the room. Perhaps this is what educators call an inter-disciplinary lesson. I enjoyed it. I should have mentioned the phagocytes.

We also discussed the passing on of disease through blood, which came back to bite me when one student said, "I told you Macbeth was going to get sick from killing Duncan." Perplexed, I asked him how. He continued confidently, "He is going to commit a murder by following instructions covered in blood, so Duncan must have some sort of disease, and when he is killed, the blood that spurts out on the instructions will then be touched by Macbeth and his wife, which will give them both the plague."

While this answer was absolutely off the mark, I really appreciated the kid's effort to explain the passage. Here I inserted, "Well, let's continue and see if you are right." That is teacher code for, "In the next few minutes you will find out how wrong you are, but I don't want to say anything negative to you because you are one of three students who will attempt to answer questions in here, and I will need your comments in the future to let me know I am not alone inside these walls."

I never complain about students who try. Thank God for them. I just hope they keep the wrong answers coming, because, for a teacher as for a radio talk show host, dead air is death, and people will change the channel. Talk about something, and you might find them tuned in.

At the very least, they know how to find page numbers, but even that task can get problematic. *Frankenstein's* chapters are numbered with Roman numerals, so when students read that, they might as well be trying to find the cure for cancer or the location of Atlantis. The *X*s and *V*s baffle them; in fact, the people who know how to read those numerals are most often gang members. The litmus test for identifying gang members or drug dealers in the crowd is to ask questions about Roman numerals and the metric system. If a student gets them right, you should call the local authorities immediately. After all, no true, drug-free American understands grams or has any real idea what a kilo is.

I once had a student named Randall who volunteered to read aloud once all year when I described the part of the apothecary in *Romeo and Juliet*. This drug dealer sells Romeo the dram of poison he uses in the final act of the play. I had found a willing reader:

Randall's hand went straight up for that part. All of the other students snickered.

The next year, when he was a sophomore, his car parked on campus was raided, and in it were discovered more drugs than Shakespeare's apothecary had in his whole shop. I received an e-mail from a fellow teacher that announced succinctly, "Elvis has left the building." Nothing more needed to be said. We never saw Randall again.

Teenagers base their answers on what is current in their teen world. You cannot begrudge them thinking that there is a drunk girl running around a clothing shop at the close of the first act when Lady Macbeth says, "Was hope drunk wherein you dressed yourself?" as she rebukes her husband for deciding not to kill the king. The fact that *hope* is lowercase does not deter this interpretation whatsoever. Texting has revolutionized teens' grammar and spelling. Anything goes now. While there might have been a girl somewhere named Hope who enjoyed partaking of fine Scottish single malts from the Highlands, it ruins the figurative language and symbolism of a play if students don't get out of their adolescent world.

Of course, Lady Macbeth ultimately does talk her husband into killing King Duncan, and my students correctly point out that if Macbeth had listened to that drunk girl named Hope, all would have turned out well for him.

I cannot argue with that. I knew a girl in college named Hope. She certainly fit that mold.

6

NOT YOUR CHEESE

**'Faith, sir, we were carousing till the second cock:
And drink, sir, is a great provoker of three things…
…nose-painting, sleep, and urine.
Macbeth Act II**

My friends who work with adults have a hard time relating to what I do. The scariest thing for teachers is to be judged by what their students know, which is ironic, because that is about the only way to tell whether a teacher is having any impact at all.

I remember one time I was out with a group of friends, and we went to Starbucks to get a drink. When the window opened at the drive-thru, I recognized the girl working the register as a former student. She said, "Hey, Mr. Fogelstrom. I thought that was you." My friends got a kick out of the fact that she had called me *Mister*. When she returned with our order, she said, "Hey, you ain't still teaching English no more, are you?" Apparently, I never had taught her any. She also forgot to put vanilla in my mocha, which was no surprise, as she had never brought her book to class, either.

Another time, my wife and I were headed to the checkout at Target one holiday shopping evening when I spotted Danica. Now,

Danica once was a member of my low-level English class; she had struggled with just about everything. Her personality was wonderful, and I enjoyed speaking with her, but problem solving was not her forte. As we approached the various lines with the lighted numbers above them, I realized that getting into Danica's line would be a fatal flaw. I had a decision to make. Despite the fact that her line only had one person in it while the others were eight deep, I knew to avoid it. Call it teacher instinct if you will. My wife followed my lead, somewhat hesitantly, and we went to stand in the longer line.

By the time we hit the register, Danica's line had a manager and assistant manager helping her void incorrect transactions. It looked like the floor of the stock exchange. People were bustling to and fro elsewhere while her line was frozen in time. Not one person had been handed a receipt. She had locked up her whole system. My line moved quickly, and as we headed out the door, Danica saw me and yelled, "Hey, Mr. Fogelstrom!" with a big smile. I saw her brother several years later. He informed me that she was working airport security as a baggage screener. I now take the train.

Perhaps I had failed Danica at some point. Assessing students can be humbling for a teacher. At the end of the year, when students sign my yearbook as they head into summer, almost half of them write, "*Your* a great teacher." I just accept it as another example of irony for me to use in the coming years.

Community members frequently make statements like, "If teachers would just explain clearly why learning is relevant and encourage students to do their best, all problems would be solved" and "Get back to basics: teach reading, writing, and math, and all will be well." What novel ideas! If I'd just explain everything clearly with a smile on my face, along with a cookie prepared for the first student who raises a hand, all would work out swimmingly. Hmmmm. I guess I should not have been trying each day to confuse and discourage the masses. All this time, I had been taking the wrong approach.

I invite anyone in the adult world to come in and give directions for a task as simple as putting a heading on a piece of paper. This seemingly mundane operation has inherent difficulties never imagined beyond a public school's walls. It goes something like this:

Teacher: OK, students, take out a sheet of binder paper. I am going to show you how to put a proper heading on your assignments.

Student A: I don't have any paper.

Teacher: Our current school budget does not allow me to hand out paper to each student, so please bring your own paper to class from now on. Can anyone give *Student A* a piece of paper? Thank you. Now, in the top left-hand corner, I want you to write your last name first, then a comma, and then your first name.

Student A: Can I just put my first initial?

Teacher: Just write it all out, please. No initials.

Student A: I don't go by that name on your roll sheet, and my mom said that I have to use my stepdad's last name right now because we're getting my real one changed to his.

Teacher: Fine. Just remind me, and I will adjust your name in my grade book. After you have written your name, underneath that, I want you to write the name of the class and the period number. This is English Nine, so please write *English 9* and then *Period 3* next to it.

Student A: Do we need a comma between the two?

Teacher: *No*, just write them side by side.

Student A: Which side of the page are we on?

Teacher: The left side, at the top.

Student A: Is that above or below the line I see?

Teacher: We will write the heading above that line within the one-inch margin space provided.

Student A: What's a margin?

Student B: I think it's a type of butter or something.

Teacher: *No. Margarine* is what you are thinking of there. A *margin* is the edge of the text on your paper. Typically,

	your paper will have one-inch margins on all sides in accordance with MLA standards.
Student A:	What's MLA?
Student C:	I think that's the group of missing soldiers in Vietnam. I saw a movie about them. Hella good. Rambo was an MLA for a while, I think.
Teacher:	*No,* you are thinking of *MIA. MLA* stands for Modern Language Association. Let's get back to the heading, OK? Now, beneath the class and the period, you are to write the date. Just write the day, the month, and then the year. I have it listed on the board behind me for you visual learners. In fact, the entire heading is there on the board, but I know some of you are confused because it does not look like a piece of paper.
Student C:	That would be cool.
Teacher:	What?
Student C:	That would be hella cool if they made a whiteboard that looked like a lined piece of paper.
Student D:	Hecka dumb. How would they punch three holes in it?
Teacher:	All right! This is taking a bit longer than I had anticipated. Now, any questions about the date?
Student E:	Yeah, can we abbreviate the date?
Teacher:	Just write it out. It will always be the day the paper is due, got it? That way, you know when the assignment is due.
Student D:	But what if I am absent?
Student A:	I still need a piece of paper.

Such scenarios can generate entire bookfuls of "what-ifs." And even after all of the questions are answered, the class is still confused. The top students finish their headings before I open my mouth once they look at the board and see what's coming. The B students have their headings done once they realize what I'm going to ask them with my use of the words, "Put your heading on a piece of paper." Both groups finish the task in under a minute and then grow bored as the rest try to catch up.

The average students sort of get it as I walk them through each step. About two-thirds of their headings are done correctly. The poor students write their first names and maybe attempt the year part of the date requirement. The failing students don't have paper—ever—or draw pictures in the margin instead of the requested heading on paper I eventually give them out of sympathy.

You wonder how these kids ever survive in the real world. I went to Car Quest once to buy a blinker light for my Toyota. The girl behind the counter was failing my class at the time. I was scared to death to have her order my part, but I figured, "Hey, each person has a set of special skills. This young lady is probably a great worker here and most likely knows her stuff. So what if she doesn't do her homework or comprehend Shakespeare? She probably knows brake parts like nobody's business."

She banged away at her computer and then asserted, "Your part will be here in seven days." I received a phone call from Car Quest a week later and went to get my new blinker light. I arrived and an employee wheeled out a box as tall as I am. As we opened it, we soon discovered she had ordered the entire front grill of my model, with headlights, fog lamps, lower-grill spoiler, and the blinker. At school, I would have given her a passing grade of D because the blinker did arrive, and it was on time. A grade of D in the real world puts a company out of business or causes a roof to collapse. It doesn't really cut it.

I wish someone would create a nice rubric assessment for every job. Wouldn't it be fun to see how you ranked and how your employer was going to modify the business world just for you? I was in the library this year doing research with my students when several kids wandered in from Spanish class. They were there—and I am not making this up—to find nacho recipes on the Internet. They all had official passes. How, exactly, does a teacher grade that one? Here is a possible rubric from that language class.

Nacho Rubric Form: Student Name_____

A: Chips, Cheese, Sour Cream (Guacamole also accepted) and one meat item (Beef, Chicken, Pork)

B: Chips, Cheese, and one other item. (If meat item is named, then bump grade to a B+. All other items = B)

C: Chips and Cheese

D: Chips or Cheese

F: No Chips / No Cheese / Recipe for another food item

It was ironic that the Spanish teacher sent students to find a nacho recipe, since nachos originated in American ballparks as snacks at baseball games.

And, speaking of irony...after a momentary mental break and refocus session at my desk, I jumped into scene six to introduce every English teacher's favorite literary term. Upon arriving at Inverness, King Duncan exclaims, "This castle hath a pleasant seat, the air nimbly and sweetly recommends itself unto our gentle senses." Since we have just labored though Lady Macbeth's affair with the blind priest and her child's murder by breast, I feel I should take the helm firmly to steer the crew through the nasty literary storm known as irony.

"OK, we just finished a scene in which Lady Macbeth made her intentions known regarding the murder of King Duncan. She told her husband that he should "Look like th' innocent flower, but be the serpent under it." Why are Duncan's words ironic as he approaches the castle of Mr. and Mrs. Macbeth?" Waving hands. I must finally be reaching them. "Yes? Explain the irony in this situation."

One student loudly contributes, "Are the Disneyland Grad Night tickets on sale yet?"

Another: "No, they go on sale next week at the student store."

A third: "Man, that's hella expensive right after the senior ball."

Many join the discussion, and the general consensus is that while Disneyland is fun, it's not worth all the cash it will require of them for Senior Grad Night. Plus, they loathe all of the rules involved with dress code and behavior; I typically let them know they will end up in Mickey Jail if they cause trouble on the trip, but I do reassure them it is the "happiest jail on earth" (if that is any consolation).

Not to miss a moment to make a solid connection, I continue, "Since Disneyland is known as the 'happiest place on earth,' what could happen there that would create an ironic situation?" Dagger looks are directed my way for having turned Disneyland into an opportunity to teach something academic. Students absolutely hate this.

I once tried to connect *The Lord of the Rings* with William Wordsworth's poem "The Excursion" and the Industrial Revolution. It was a fantastic lesson with great relevance and connections to historical and literary events. At the close, a student blurted out, "Great! The next thing you know, he's going to ruin *Star Wars*, too!"

I countered, "I'll try not to, but *Star Wars* can relate to Sophocles's tragedy *Oedipus* and has tons of connections to the hero's journey archetype found in mythology."

They laughed at me derisively and exclaimed, "Yeah, right!"

I finished, "Luke Skywalker had a love interest with a member of his own family in the first movie, and ultimately, whom does he attempt to kill?"

A hand went up in the back of the room. "Luke tried to kill his own father, similar to Oedipus, who killed Laius." My learners were devastated. I guess the world is a horrible place when you are forced to think that events are actually connected. There really is nothing new.

I watched one kid absolutely light up when I brought up the term *archetypes*. We were covering *The Iliad*, and I explained that Achilles "retired" to his ships for most of the epic and was not directly involved in the war. He refused to fight until his friend Patroclus went into battle and was slain by Hector. Achilles came "out of retirement," reentered the war, and had an epic duel with Hector. It was the first great one-on-one battle recorded in literature. When I had completed my summary, a student yelled, "Hey, they stole that from *Rocky IV!*" Come to think of it, perhaps Homer did have a time machine, and, feeling stressed for material, came to Los Angeles in the 1980s to plagiarize Stallone's script. Who knows?

Students sometimes are not even sure why things are funny. As parents, we try to give our children a degree of cultural literacy, because anything confusing is typically explained by relating it to something that is common knowledge. What do you do, though, when there is no knowledge at all? With my infant child, I held up an item and kept naming it to build her schema. Perhaps that is the key to classroom success.

Should I do that in class all period? If I use the phrase "don't cry wolf" as an allusion but the student doesn't get what I am saying, I am forced to explain the fable of "The Boy Who Cried Wolf." No eighteen-year-old should have to listen to that story, but what is one to do? In the end, they stare blankly, wondering what a wolf has to do with anything. When a student is being less than truthful and I respond, "Your nose is growing," do I share the story of Pinocchio to show that lies build on lies, or do I allow that student to actually rush out of the room and look in a mirror to assess nose growth? "Pinocchio" is not found in the state content standards, so I'm afraid I would have to skip it.

If I were to share these stories to provide background for some of the allusions in *Macbeth*, sadly, students' minds would blend together Greeks, Pinocchio, Shakespeare, and some random thought running around in their heads. At least a third of the students would be perplexed as to why a wolf and a Greek boy were part of Shakespeare's play, or why a puppet and a cricket were in Scotland discussing nose rings. They would question why some Greek kid had a job in the fields without a work permit. Furthermore, they would ponder why a kid would even want a job in the farming industry when he could be employed at Chuck E Cheese and get "hella tokens" for free.

Like lint rollers, students have to pass over the same material again and again to pick it all up. Some have stickier surfaces than others, and some just keep rearranging the lint and hair. What is really scary, though, is what they do pick up sometimes. In *Romeo and Juliet*, the character Mercutio delivers an image-filled speech about dreams and what causes them. He describes intricately a fairy queen named Mab. During my review session on *Romeo and Juliet*, I asked my ninth graders, "Who gave the dream speech in the play?"

A student raised his hand and answered, "Martin Luther King."

It's nice to know that retention is not entirely a myth; kudos to the History Department for that one. Now, if I could just get an answer within a hundred years of Shakespeare, I would have hope for the future.

I can't be too harsh on today's students, though. Several years ago, I walked into a football meeting only to hear a coach say, "Badges? We don't need no stinkin' badges," to which I responded, "*Blazing Saddles*. Great and freakin' hilarious movie." The coach was a guy in his fifties who said I didn't even know why that line was funny in *Blazing Saddles*. I stared at him the way my students stare at me.

Two minutes later, another coach my age came in and endured the same humiliation.

Another few minutes went by, and our veteran coach, who was about sixty, walked in. When he was quoted the line, he smiled and reminisced, "*The Treasure of the Sierra Madre*. What a great movie!"

I had failed the parody test. I just thought the line was funny in and of itself. I was clueless, though. I try to remember that moment when I get frustrated in class. Someone has to tell the kids this kind of stuff, and that is what I've been charged with in life.

After I'd walked students through the process of studying irony, a student in the front felt comfortable enough to throw out his answer about the term's application to our Disneyland venture: "If you got left home from Disneyland, that would be ironic."

Trying to see his point and trusting in the goodness of teenagers and the learning process, I asked, "How does not going to Disneyland create an ironic situation?"

Grimacing with frustrated annoyance, he retorted, "'Cause."

It seems that, in my student's eyes, this monosyllabic term sufficed as a quality support beam for most any argument. I have often wanted to give the same explanation to the IRS or my mortgage bank. In the magical world of teenagers, "'cause" is seen as sufficient reason for any behavior.

Another hand went up. Eerily, it was that of the same student who had answered the *Star Wars* versus *Oedipus* question.

"Mr. Fogelstrom, if a student went to Disneyland, tripped, and fell, was taken to the medical center on site for a blood transfusion, and upon receiving this blood transfusion came into contact with the HIV virus, then I would consider that ironic because something horrible and sad happened at the 'happiest place on earth.' Furthermore, if that person then left the medical building with blood still seeping from the wound and hugged her friends for support, that act of hugging, which shows friendship and love, could actually transmit the virus again and again, thus creating a catastrophic AIDS outbreak at Disneyland known as the Mickey Plague, and perhaps an example of situational irony more profound than any seen since Oedipus cursed himself dozens of times."

Dead silence.

I looked at my roll sheet.

"I know you just transferred in here. Where are you from?" I asked. All eyes turned to the back of the room.

"Yes, I came from over the hill. I was in Advanced Placement English."

"Over the hill" was code for living in a higher socioeconomic area. I knew the area. I also knew what I had to do, instantly. I summarily called the student up to my desk, gave her a pass to the office, explained that AP English was down the hall, and that she would do well to get a schedule change. She smiled, picked up her backpack (which actually contained books rather than candy or crack), and headed out the door, carrying with her 80 percent of the total intelligence quotient that had been in my room.

"Mr. Fogelstrom, what was she talking about?" groaned a large portion of the class.

Trying to recover from actually hearing an intelligent, well-thought-through answer, I just stuttered, "I...I don't know, kids. She was in the wrong room. Remember the earlier comment about irony and being left home from Disneyland? Well, that could be ironic in some situations, I suppose." The one student who had earlier contributed the erroneous example nodded his head in an affirmative manner to let me know he was with me on this one despite my complete knowledge that I had failed to teach irony to anyone and the only student who knew it had just walked out of my room forever.

You have to understand your students before you can reach any of them. During my second year of teaching, I had an ESL teacher escort a boy into my room who had just come from Mexico and who appeared to speak little or no English, though the instructor suspected otherwise. Apparently, the student had not bought into the quiet atmosphere and calm approach of the ESL class, so he was sent to regular English with me. Jorge was actually wearing a serape with the Mexican flag's colors when he came to my room. I asked him why he didn't have his textbook, and he replied with a thick accent, "Too heavy." We were off and running with that bit of information.

I guess the teacher was right: he did speak English. I remembered passing the ESL class a couple of days earlier and hearing the kids break down daily oral language assignments like a bunch of linguists and grammarians. The teacher kept mostly girls from Mexico who had attended elite private schools there. It was like an honors English class for Hispanic girls. If an immigrant student truly needed help but was disruptive in any way, she farmed him out to the main population, claiming he spoke English "just fine" and would pass. Perhaps

I should have bought Jorge a set of weights or a lighter text to spark a successful transition into my room.

Jorge and I came to an understanding. He became my tardy monitor: he'd stand at my door, "encouraging" students to show up on time or the class would go out late to lunch. In return for this service, I provided him with a textbook each day. He was learning the American business system in eighth grade. I think he works at Walmart now, greeting customers with his clipboard of smiley-face stickers.

In junior high, try to get the biggest kids on your side. I had two Samoan brothers in my last-period eighth-grade class one year. One had a full beard. I asked them if they were twins, but they told me they were two years apart. I didn't pursue why they were both in eighth grade at the same time, because I was afraid to hear the answer.

In October, they disappeared for six months and then showed up again one April day.

When I asked where they had been, the bearded one responded succinctly, "On vacation." I made him my "quiet monitor": if my last-period students got too loud, I would detain them after school. This massive eighth grader, who obviously wanted to get out of school on time so he could go home and pack for his next six-month vacation, would just turn and look at the class if anyone got loud at all. I think they all got the point pretty fast. Instantly, they'd close their collective mouths. I hope I never got any "talker" hurt in the lunch yard.

It's amazing how effective peer-to-peer instruction can be.

7

TWO BEES OR NOT TWO BEES

Were such things here as we do speak about?
Or have we eaten on the insane root
That takes the reason prisoner?
Macbeth Act I

W hen I moved to high school, I taught a study skills class one period a day. Teachers selected several students they thought would be successful in a small class environment that moved at a slower pace. It was designed to help those kids who were focused on passing their classes but needed a little more organization. Most of the teachers saw this as an excellent opportunity to remove their discipline problems from their regular class population. It happens all of the time, better believe!

The study skills class was my introduction to learning disabilities and modifications. Every single student in the room was on a 504 plan, an individualized education plan (IEP), or was in the process of testing with potential for a resource or special-education learning environment. A typical day ran like this:

Mr. F: OK, class, let's get out the homework from math, science, English, and history.

Student X: We don't have any.

Mr. F:	How can you possibly have no homework from all four core classes?
Student X:	Scoobiddydoo, scoobydoo!
Mr. F:	Huh?
Student Y:	Ramone doing that all day. Hella dumb!
Student X:	Scoobiddydoo, scoobydoo, scoobiddy—
Mr. F:	Stop! I appreciate the effort to make onomatopoetic sounds, but it is distracting.
Student X:	He said *onamana*! Hecka funny!
Student Z:	Mr. Fogie [that's my nickname], I got that assignment from last class that we worked on in groups.
Mr. F:	Thanks. Let me make sure all of your names are on it. Hey, why does it say "Walking S" at the top of the page?
Student Z:	He in our group.
Mr. F:	Walking S? What is that?
Student Z:	Him. That dude...you callin' him "Walking" all the time.
Mr. F:	No, his name is *Joaquin*, not *Walking*. His name is Joaquin Sanchez.
Student Q:	What's a Walking Sanchez?
Mr. F:	Probably a poisonous spider found in Mexico. But...
	(Noise: rhythmic banging on a desk.)
Student X:	Three pigs in a bucket, Mother, mother f— it!
	(Laughter all around.)
Mr. F:	Nice couplet there, but watch your epithets.
Student X:	Epi-what?
Mr. F:	Epithets. They are descriptive phrases. We refer to them as curse words, but originally they were used in epic poetry.
	(*Bang!*)
Student Y:	Give me my Starbursts!
Mr. F:	What is the problem here?
Student Y:	Rick gots my Starbursts and Skittles and won't give them back.

Mr. F: Rick, give Trey back his candy. And by the way, there is no eating in class. You guys need to get along.

Student X: Hey, y'all, break bread, like Jesus said.

Mr. F: Better couplet that time, Ramone. Thanks for leaving out the curse words. Rick, Jesus wants you to give Trey back his candy.

Student Z: I ain't got his candy. He's hella stupid.

Mr. F: No one is hella stupid in here. (Pause.) And if you have his candy, give it back.

Back Row: Hella bees!

Mr. F: What?

Back Row: Hella bees outside this window.

Student X: Yeah, they flyin' all over at lunch. You can die from them stinging you.

Student Y: You hella dumb. Bees can't kill you.

Mr. F: *Stop*! Actually, if you are allergic to bees, one could kill you. Now, get out your homework.

(Students begin taking out their books and assignments, albeit reluctantly.)

(*Ding! Ding! Ding!*)

Mr. F: Here we go. This is a fire drill. Take all of your books, candy, and concerns about bees outside to the back parking lot.

Student Y: Hella hot out there, Mr. F.

Mr. F: Yes, it is pretty hot out. Hey, Rick, I just saw you take Trey's candy off his desk. Come here.

(I search Rick. He empties about twenty dollars' worth of candy from the seventeen pockets he has between his jacket and his parachute pants.)

Student Q: I told you—Rick steals.

Mr. F: Let's move, guys. We need to get to the back parking lot.

Back Row: I don't wanna go.

Mr. F: Why?

Back Row: Hella bees!

This goes on and on until the bell rings for next period.

If you lack a sense of humor, get out of teaching. Nothing can prepare you for dealing with bees, Skittles, and thieves. To this day, my favorite study-skills-type kid is known as "Gum on My Shoe."

Gum on My Shoe was in high school but appeared to be about ten years old. He wore thick glasses, Atari 2600 T-shirts, and found any class with more than a dozen students to be a reason for anxiety. I first met him while subbing in another class. The class contained just six students, and Gum on My Shoe was not there when I took roll. When I asked for him, one student in the class said, "Oh, he'll be here. He's just always late."

Tardies in most classes are fairly serious, but I was beginning to realize that this was a unique bunch, and while geometry was the subject of the course, I knew I was in quite a different room from the norm. I looked out the window, and there I saw Gum on My Shoe crossing the quad. He was throwing his hands wildly into the air and muttering things to the heavens, so I figured this had to be my guy. I opened the door and said, "Joshua, hurry up, buddy. Class has started."

Of course, I was a sub that period and he did not have a clue who I was, but he stopped immediately in the middle of the quad and yelled, "I have gum on my shoe!" I have to admit that I hate having gum on my shoe, but rarely is it cause for panic. However, this young lad's world was rocked to its core by a stick of Wrigley's Spearmint affixed to his sneaker. I walked over to him and told him to sit down on the bench. I wanted to see what I could do to help. The gum was wedged in there pretty good.

Now, I had a room of five or so kids sitting by themselves while I attempted to clean gum off this kid's shoe. I told him to wait just a second while I found something to clean it up with. I went back into the room, and the kids were just sitting there. No one was talking or moving. I asked one student near the door, "Is Joshua always like this?"

The kid said with absolutely no emotion, "Yesterday he flipped out because he could feel the heat coming off the overhead projector." Now I knew exactly what world I was living in.

I looked all over the room for something to clean the gum from this shoe, but it wasn't my room, so I didn't want to mess up scissors or rulers or anything else in there. I looked out the door and spied an old tree. I headed outside again, propped the door open so I could actually see the kids in class, and then broke a small branch off a tree. I raced over to the bench to clean Josh's shoe. He had rolled himself up into a stress ball while I looked for gum-removal equipment. It was hot that day, and I was starting to sweat like crazy while digging with a stick into the tread of his sneaker. Josh was in a panic. I heard one kid from inside the class say, "Hey, this teacher's breaking tree branches!" They all rushed to the door to see what I was doing to the tree.

I soon became aware that I was getting absolutely nowhere in terms of removing gum from this kid's shoe. Tired, sweaty, and deeply concerned that no geometry was getting done, I formulated a new plan in my head. "Joshua, you are going to need to take your shoe off. The gum will dry out here in the sun [doubtful] and then we can clean it up after class." He took off his shoe, gave it to me, and then started toward the door. I noticed he was limping as he walked.

I asked him what was wrong, and he said, "I can still feel the gum." At this point, I wanted to just get back into class and try to get this lesson going. And there was no way in hell I was going to turn on the overhead projector after hearing about yesterday's fiasco. Gum *plus* the overhead projector's heat would just be too much for this kid to handle in one day.

When we walked into the room, Gum on My Shoe suddenly froze in the doorway. All the kids were staring at him. He was wearing only one shoe, and I still had a tree branch in my hand, which made us look like some of Malcolm's soldiers storming Macbeth's castle in Act V while holding up branches from Birnam Wood. (I need to remember that illustration for my seniors.) We were quite the scene.

Gum on My Shoe exploded with rage and yelled, "You, you, you don't know what it's like to have gum on your shoe! All of you, you, you, you probably leave your gum on the ground all over school so people like me will step in it. It's all your fault!" This was getting serious now. I stopped Gum on My Shoe's tirade and told him to get to his seat so we could get going and start measuring some angles or anything geometrically related. We were getting close now to starting the lesson.

He limped over to his chair but stopped again. It was obvious that something was welling up inside the young man, and he took his backpack and threw it down on the ground as hard as he could, which really wasn't that hard, because the kid could not have weighed more than ninety pounds. Still, it made a loud noise, and then he continued on his anti-gum crusade: "You, you, you are all criminals. Leaving gum on the ground is vandalism. It's vandalism. In fact, you are all vandals! *Vandals!*"

At this point, Gum on My Shoe was bright red and sweating, and his glasses had fogged up. I stopped him again and said, "OK, time to go to the office with me. You cannot call people criminals. That's slander. Plain and simple slander. You don't want to be a slanderer." I then caught myself. Much like Macbeth's slow slide into the speech patterns of the witches, I was starting to speak like Gum on My Shoe. This had to end immediately.

He stood there, frozen. Perhaps *slander* was a cool, new word to him that he could use in his next accusatory speech against his peers. I believe the cry, "You're all slanderers!" might fit nicely with Gum on My Shoe's chosen diction.

We headed across the quad in the hot sun, Gum on My Shoe with one sneaker on and an exposed sock, and I trying to maintain my composure. When we got to the office, I took him to the counselor for a little therapy time. She is a friend of mine who is great with kids. I told her that Joshua was having a bad day and that he needed a task or two in the office to get his mind right again. She obliged, and as I walked back to class, I heard her say, "Oh, honey, what happened to your other shoe?" I don't think she wanted to hear the answer to that one.

Such experiences have made me the teacher I am today. My parents used to say that I had no patience. That defect in my character has been remedied due to hours of playing ringmaster in such circuses.

8

ALL THE WORLD'S A STAGE

Thou sure and firm-set earth,
Hear not my steps, which way they walk, for fear
Thy very stones prate of my whereabout,
And take the present horror from the time,
Which now suits with it.

Macbeth Act II

If students can drive a teacher crazy, Lady Macbeth is a dead ringer for the student body. Students point out that Lady Macbeth practically nags her husband into killing Duncan. If you watch the Polanski film, you sympathize with Macbeth when he has to deal with the high-pitched whining of his wife. Such nasality of voice would definitely drive most husbands nuts.

Try eating in a teacher lunchroom sometime, and you will feel for Scotsman Macbeth, who drowned in his wife's negativity. Teachers, you see, are born complainers. I do it all of the time myself. The inclination to complain diminishes if one begins his or her teaching career in the worst situation possible—at the bottom level. If I were to write my teacher biography, it would start with the following line:

*I began my teaching career in a small, southern town in
northern California...*

It sounds like a bad opening to an ever-worsening book, but it is most
accurate. I owe the phrasing to a history teacher I admired. After a
blessed student teaching experience at a high school where they hired
people to type tests and make copies for the faculty, I took a contrast-
ing position in the Drama Department at a junior high for my first
real teaching job. Actually, I *was* the Drama Department. That was
the only positive facet of the job: I could hold my one-person department meetings while sipping a soda in my car on the way home from
work. In my present job, having once been a drama teacher, I don't
have high expectations when it comes to student oral interpretations
of *Macbeth*. I have been there and done that.

I was informally introduced to the person I was to replace when I
arrived during the summer to prepare my broom-closet-sized "office"
behind the stage in the cafeteria. She was cleaning out her materials
and met me with, "So, they tricked you into working here, huh? Good
luck. This place is hell." It was not the motivating speech I might have
wished for, but it did inspire me to take an approach based on the
presupposition: *These kids just haven't had a positive teacher before. I am
going to develop strong relationships with them to set them on fire and make
them love the theater.*

On the stage in the cafeteria, I taught students who were not sure
why they were even enrolled in drama. My class was part of what educators call "an exploratory wheel." That meant that I did not have any
students who were in foreign language, band, choir, leadership, or
any other courses that required critical thinking and organization.
The focus of administrators was always, "These kids are high-spirited
[a euphemism for *disruptive*], and drama will provide an ideal outlet
where they can express themselves."

This was a truism: they certainly did express themselves. I found
out that they had worn out three drama teachers the previous year.
The positive light I had met at the drama office that summer had

only worked there for a half of the previous year before the high-spirited young leeches had sucked her dry.

Still, meeting her was better than when I first met the metal and wood shop teachers. The metal shop teacher ran into me in the parking lot, literally, because he was focused on the ground ahead of his feet while muttering to himself, "Damn kids. Something was going on. I know it!" After he regained his wits (if that was even possible after thirty years in junior high welding), he let me in on his turmoil. "See this videotape? I am taking this home. Got cameras all over my room. Something was happening in the back during sixth period. I'll get 'em. Got the whole place covered."

I remember that I then sneezed several times in a row because he commented, "Got allergies, huh? Ever since I started these anti-depressants, I haven't had a lick of trouble with allergies. Great side effect." If I had the choice between allergies or paranoia with dilated pupils, I guess I would stick with the Kleenex as my personal remedy.

Soon after running into the metal shop teacher, the wood shop teacher introduced himself to me as "Coach So-and-So." I am not a trained psychologist, but bells go off in my head when a wood shop teacher calls himself "Coach." Apparently, Coach Woodshop had been laboring under the delusion that he was coaching student athletes in how to make birdhouses and doorstops. I later found out he had never been a coach of any kind at any school at any level, but that didn't stop him from using the gridiron to get his points across to the youngsters.

For the first three months that I taught drama, he called my room several times to suggest a football game between our classes. I realized that I would have a hard time justifying to parents that we were tossing the pigskin around in drama class, and, as a first-year teacher, I was concerned about where such an activity would fit in with my curriculum and objectives. Furthermore, a teacher's first two years are "probationary," which means one can be released for any reason. I figured that playing football outside during drama period might be one cause for dismissal.

As the quarter drew to a close, I realized that I could not damage my students any more than many of them already had been. I figured no one would complain as their parents hadn't responded to any of the progress reports sent home, so I agreed to play a game of football under the guise that it was a transition day for my students before they left my class for the next elective on the wonder wheel.

The drama class versus the wood shop class. What a battle!

I sold it to the kids with the promise that they were going to earn extra credit if we won. I offered ten points for a victory and five for participation. As a typical quarter was worth around a thousand points, this extra-credit offer was about one-hundredth of a percent of the grade. We are talking fractions here.

The beautiful thing about students is that, to them, the concept of percentages is a mystery rivaling those of the Sphinx, Stonehenge, and the ancient aliens theory. Many honestly believe that they can take an entire quarter off but that the lucky spreadsheet will calculate a passing grade for them if they have a paltry ten points of extra credit. Even many of my seniors in high school hope for this same miracle. Kids really do believe in Santa Claus.

Many of my drama students were confused, just as I had been, about why we were playing football against wood shop during a regular class period. I led my students down the hall toward the shop classrooms. I assured them it was all standard procedure at the end of the quarter and that all would be well.

I walked those kids into an ambush that day. The door opened to the wood shop class, where my eyes beheld thirty or so junior high students wearing red jerseys. I thought, *My God, what do they do in here? Do they sew as well as hammer and saw?* Coach Woodshop, complete with jersey and cleats on, was in the back of the room, warming up. He looked as though he had done this before. "Do you need to get loose?" he asked.

"I'm fine," I replied, though I was far from it at that point.

Apparently, he expected me to play, too, as he was wearing a quarterback jersey with his name on it. All of a sudden, I wished I had listened to the advice of several other teachers. They had told me not to do this, but like a young fool or Macbeth blinded with ambition, I had ignored all warnings. It was a typical rookie mistake. Coach Woodshop, who had now become Quarterback Woodshop, announced to both of our classes, "Please have a seat, and pay attention to the ground rules for today's game."

His students jumped to their seats while he threw a series of five-yard passes to his designated warm-up team in the back of the room between the belt sander and the vise grips. Then he turned and hit the remote control. All of a sudden, a fifty-inch television came on, and there on the screen in full color was a video of Coach Woodshop giving directions. The volume blared, "Welcome, student athletes! Today we are going to play the greatest game America has given the world…football! There will be some ground rules you need to follow. We will play touch football…"

And so it continued. I felt like I was in the *Twilight Zone*. Needless to say, as his team charged the field, mine just sort of oozed into their positions, which we were still working out as the game began. He yelled, "First-string offense!" and I swear on my grandma's grave, they sprinted out and formed a huddle where Coach Woodshop barked out the plays in code. They had their own plays!

They approached the line of scrimmage, and "Coach," a middle-aged shop teacher, actually took a hike from a female center, and the man was not in shotgun formation. That was enough right there to blow the horn, call the game, and put his picture on the front page of the local newspaper. I kept thinking, *I'm going to get sued somehow for this fiasco! At the bare minimum, I will be seeking other employment by the end of this day. This can't be right.*

Years later, Coach Woodshop was transferred elsewhere because a dad showed up at school a tad furious about his daughter being made to snap a football to a wood shop teacher with his hands on her rear. As he walked off campus, some kid yelled, "Hey, take a hike, coach!" I found that line filled with Shakespearean wit and tucked it into my memory for later use when discussing irony and double entendres.

The only saving grace of that day was a student named Shawn, who was a nightmare for all of his core teachers. This kid never stopped talking or moving. I figured that since I was soon going to be out of a job and on the cover of the local paper for playing football during drama class plus being a witness to a quarterback molesting a center, I might as well go down in flames. Every single play was, "Shawn, go deep." I made that kid run about six thousand yards' worth of sprints in forty minutes. By the end of the period, he could hardly breathe. The bell rang, and I sent him off to English class.

The rest of his teachers never found out why Shawn had his most focused day of the year in their academic courses that day. I heard comments in the lunchroom about how well behaved he had been for the first time that year but that he had come to class rather smelly and sweaty. Maybe wind sprints should be required before school for all junior high students. It's a thought, at least.

Years later, I saw Shawn again. By a bizarre twist of fate, his attention deficit disorder (ADD) and oppositional defiant disorder (ODD) had disappeared when his parents sent him off to military school. He greeted me with, "Hello, sir," and told me his goals for the future. Somehow, I like to think it all started with, "Shawn, go deep!" and his near–cardiac arrest during drama class vertical-pass routes.

We were slaughtered that day, and I think Coach Woodshop spent time hanging a banner in his room the next afternoon, claiming division title rights for the first-quarter Wood Shop and Drama passing league. I swear he had little kids with headsets on the roof radioing down the defensive fronts and offensive formations. Later that year, a student broke his collarbone during one of the games, which had to be an intra-wood-shop scrimmage because no one would play him anymore. A mom showed up at school wanting to know how her son could break a bone or get tackled by another student while making a picture frame. Sadly, I knew the answer. Watching "Coach," I learned a great many things not to do as a teacher; moreover, I spent my first year observing everyone I could just to see how the world of teaching works and what methods created success and stability.

My drama office faced the band room. I grew to appreciate my job as the drama teacher each day during my prep when I saw the band director trying to harness thirty seventh and eighth graders to a sheet of music. One day, I thought he must have quit, as chaos reigned in his room. Kids were blowing cornets in each other's ears; one young man was trying to play the drums with his head; another tiny kid was sitting in a cymbal like it was a snow saucer preparing to go down a ski run, and no one was seated.

I headed over to stop the mayhem but then noticed through my office window that the teacher was writing this sentence on the board: "If we all get together, we can play beautiful music, but if this chaos continues, each and every one of you will write this very, very long sentence at least one hundred times, and that number may continue to grow for every minute it takes to get you in your seats and…"

It was like someone had injected each kid with an adrenaline shot of reason. They ran to their seats, took their music out, and by the time the band director turned to face the class, they were model citizens poised to express the magic of Mozart with their rented flutes and chipped drumsticks. This was a man who knew junior high students. I watched in awe and took mental notes.

I used to sub in his class occasionally when he took a sanity day. I pretended I knew what I was doing. We just played fight songs from schools such as Notre Dame and Michigan. The hilarious part was that we were a multitrack, year-round school at the time, which meant that during each month, one-fourth of the students were on vacation. If you really want to destroy an elective program and put your arts teachers on psychiatric drugs, just make them work under this system. Put a band together in that situation, and you are my hero.

We would be going along fine in a song when the room would go eerily silent. I would say, "Hey, why did you guys stop?"

They would respond, "The flutes are all off track this month." We would hum for a few measures, pretending to be flutes. Once in a while, a horn would toot or a cymbal would clang, but nothing like music emerged for long sections of the symphony. During these moments, I cherished the cafeteria stage. One can replace kids in a drama scene or commercial video, but nobody can edit in the missing bass or violin sections.

You haven't lived until you have taught drama in the cafeteria. Each day at lunchtime, the nacho bar would roll through my class. That was the signal to every prepubescent child to stop learning and think about lunch.

Each assembly day at the school meant I had to switch my classes every period from free classroom to free classroom. We held drama class several times a semester in the science lab. "OK, kids, let's act like scientists today and blow something up in here." It was a nightmare.

I grew to love the only teaching resource I was given when I was hired: the video camera. We made commercials, music videos, and anything else I could come up with. I guess I impressed people, because the newspaper covered my class twice that year, and I spoke at the California League of Middle Schools convention on how to connect your "wheel" class with the regular classroom curriculum. A core group of teachers came alongside me and took me under their wing. I flew down with all of them to the conference, and they truly saved my life that year. Mentors exist in every job and are especially critical to new teachers. Teaching is one place you cannot go it alone and survive.

That's the beauty of the profession: everyone's desperately trying to figure out what works. After only two months in teaching, I was on a plane to Los Angeles to tell everyone about the wonders I was working in my class, while in reality I was leaving my job each day wondering what the heck I was doing in there and how I could apply the video learning tool to tomorrow's lesson.

I also learned that the school district would not reimburse a "Mickey meal" purchased at Disneyland but that I could turn in as many receipts as I wanted from the Hilton lounge bar with no questions asked.

The convention was interesting on many different levels, but the capper of the weekend had to be the session entitled, "How to Discipline with Watercolors." I distinctly remember the absurd method of discipline espoused. Instead of assigning detention or paragraph writing, this teacher had students express their rule-breaking behavior through watercolor painting. If I were to do that, I think the only color I'd make available would be black. There may have been something to it, though. I had a kid in junior high who drew two pictures on the back of an exam. The first was of the globe with a banner around it that read "F— the world!" The second was of the school in flames with a smiley-faced stick figure standing in front of it holding what looked like a torch.

This budding artist chronically found himself late to class. His daily excuse was that he had to Rollerblade against the wind. While I am not a meteorologist, I think the wind speed and direction vary occasionally, but this guy was still late by ten minutes every day. So, with the accumulation of tardies and two nice pictures on an exam as ammunition, I wrote a referral on the young man. I sat in on this meeting with the vice-principal just to enjoy the theater, which went something like this:

(For readers seeking an Elizabethan flavor, a translation follows this unversed version)

VP: Jeff, I see here that you have been tardy at least ten times.
Jeff: Yeah.
VP: What's going on, Jeff? Why are you late each day?
Jeff: I have to Rollerblade to school, and the wind slows me down.
VP: Did you ever think about leaving earlier to make sure you arrive on time?
Jeff: [Puzzled expression]
VP: We will get to the tardy issue later. I see here on an exam you have two pictures. The first one says "F— the World" Jeff, that is not appropriate for school. Weren't you supposed to be taking this test? I see the other side is totally blank.
Jeff: I didn't read the book. I never checked one out.
VP: Why not?

Jeff: It makes my backpack too heavy. I already get to school late. It will be worse if my backpack is heavy.*
  *How can anyone argue against logic like that?

VP: Well, my biggest concern here is the fact that you have the school in flames and a stick figure holding a torch. I will tell you what. If we have a fire at this school, I will definitely have you brought in, and this will be used as evidence.

Jeff: [Laughs and shakes his head]

VP: What is so funny, Jeff?

Jeff: You are hella stupid. That isn't a torch. That's a bomb!

Shakespearean Translation

VP: By my counting, young Geoff, thou cam'st too oft late to Fogie's, ten times in all, not less.

Geoff: Forsooth, good sir, thou strikest true the mark.

VP: Come, knave, why disturbest thou thus the peace?

Geoff: Daily do I sally forth, orbs on feet,
  Yea, but an ill-blown wind doth hinder me.

VP: Bethink me this, rogue: has thou not conceived
  Some manner by which thou might'st make remedy?

Geoff: [Flummoxed]

VP: Yet, let us broach this hindrance anon.
     Mine eyes do now fall upon thy measure,
     Wherein thou displayest images twain,
     The first bruiting "a fig to God's green world."
     Nay, Geoff, 'tis not meet for this learned realm.
     Shouldst thou not gaily besiege this measure?
     Why, thy verso doth but seem a whitewashed tomb!

Geoff: Ne'er did my eyes peruse yon testament.
  In truth, I ne'er sought to make it my own.

VP: Gadzooks, sly varlet, wherefore didst thou not?

Geoff: It doth o'erburden my rucksack, my liege.
             But late now do I reach yon hallowed halls.
             More weight would but slow my progress the more.
VP: Yet behold I here this castle in flames,
             And linéd ruffian with torch all ablaze!
             Heed well my counsel: should fiery heat reach
             This gentle vale, thy seizure shall I charge,
             And use yon sketch to charge thy soul withal.
Geoff: [Laughs, shaking head]
VP: Wherefore fallest into such a cackle?
Geoff: Fool that thou art! 'Tis not a torch thou spyest.
             Nay, 'tis a stratagem to render stone!
             O' thanks to Chinamen, whose alchemy
             Fashioned gunpowder mixed with loam!

Jeff was suspended for the week, the school never burned, the wind continued to scheme against Jeffrey's Rollerblading, and he continued to be late per his daily custom. If only I had provided some watercolors in the room, the problem might have been solved. Or, if Jeff had lived on the opposite side of town, he could have enjoyed the wind pushing him to school faster each day. This was a literal case of growing up on the wrong side of the tracks. Even the elements conspired against Jeffrey's future.

Speaking of bombs, the monotony of teaching the same curriculum five times a day can get to a teacher's sanity. I was actually happy one day when there *was* a bomb scare on campus during my prep. That meant that I could watch the explosive-disposal squad disarm the bomb, which someone had left out on the playground in a garbage can, without having to worry about one of my little actors being run over by a nacho cart or pudding tray. My prep that day ran almost three straight hours. Sweet bliss!

In the end, the bomb squad blew up this massive package, which turned out to have been a stack of porno magazines wrapped in brown paper and made to look dangerous. When the bomb team lifted the protective cover, the wind became a pornography distribution system and made every single junior high boy's dream come true that afternoon as the blast sent thousands of pictures flying around the campus. I was impressed with such an elaborate practical joke from ones so young.

Another time, some other pranksters put Crisco on all of the doorknobs on campus. All that did was finally allow my key to slide smoothly into the lock instead of getting stuck as it usually did. I actually thanked the disappointed ne'er-do-wells for that one.

After the porn bomb, someone should have checked the gifted-and-talented class for crooked smiles, giggles, and watery eyes. A confession would have been easy to extract. No average kid in the school would have parted with such dearly held magazines. As in states where the first snow of the year brings excitement to the playground, the kids had a great lunch period that day amid the porno flurries. Needless to say, keeping them focused on anything other than the naked body parts available in any tree or shrub was quite difficult. In drama class, we decided to take a trust walk that day with partners. When we got near the playground, half of my class disappeared.

My year in drama was an education in itself. Sometimes you follow every trick you were taught in the credential program, but in the end, the advice from the old educator in the corner of the teacher's lounge is more valuable than any book or professor's lecture. We'll meet that educational Zen master anon.

9

IT'S A MAD, MAD, MAD, MAD WORLD

Foul whisperings are abroad. Unnatural deeds
Do breed unnatural troubles; infected minds
To their deaf pillows will discharge their secrets;
More needs she the divine than the physician.
Macbeth Act V

Macbeth should have sought wisdom from the experienced men of Scotland, but instead he followed the bearded witches' seduction, his wife's nagging, and his own ambitions. If you have a high-functioning class, the fact that Macbeth's witches have beards creates the potential for someone to ask if they are hermaphrodites. Fortunately, that word has far too many syllables for the average high school student to tackle.

They all really get into the scene where Macbeth says, "Is this a dagger I see before me?" This makes for excellent discussion about the power of imagination and how stress can distort perception. I like to tell my students about how, as a child at Christmas, I saw Rudolph's nose in the sky and Santa's arm at my door. Both visions had been brought on by a feverish anticipation of gifts and holiday joy.

I can "birdwalk" here for at least twenty minutes by having students share about their Christmas and birthday presents and other festive occasions in their lives. Pets, vacations, and holidays are wonderful time-killing topics, too. Underclassmen always have something to share in these three areas. Seniors, though, usually just glance at the teacher and then at the clock.

The next scene in the play is the bloody murder of King Duncan, but even that brings up the color red, a holiday mainstay. Speaking of murder and mayhem, a credentialing program in college might cover some ideas related to developing classroom discussions, but it will assiduously avoid the topic of the dreaded parent-teacher conference. The art of these conferences should be studied, video recorded, analyzed, and written about, yet in all my years of college and credentialing, we never once broached this important aspect of a teacher's life.

One assumes naively that parents will be supportive. After all, if the teacher has called a conference because a student is not doing his or her assignments, there will be hell to pay at home for the student, right? I suppose teachers got that passé idea from TV shows of the 1950s, when a phone call home was enough to scare the daylights out of Johnny. Sadly, such days are ancestral mythology in the modern context.

The first thing to know about the parent-teacher conference is that whatever you are going to talk about has probably already been detailed to the parents by your colleagues. You are just the most recent link in a malfunctioning chain of events that has shackled teachers to these parents for the last decade. Early in my career, I heard about how Johnny had been doing fine until he got to this school, about how this transition to high school must be messing him up, and about how his teachers were not meeting his needs. I felt like a worm, cringing at the way I had failed my students. Here I was, the despicable teacher with the horrible lesson plans and the outdated approach to kids, responsible for single-handedly ruining the life of the child who had been so promising in younger years and in line to cure cancer or rescue kittens from high wires and burning buildings.

I started listening to the older teachers on campus. Many were burned out, but they understood the system, and they knew kids.

The old Zen master in the corner of the teacher lunchroom told me one day, "Always check the kid's cumulative folder before going into a conference." The cumulative folder contains everything about a student's school career and every school picture taken since kindergarten. Another Buddha told me, "Find the school picture where the student isn't smiling and use it as a road sign to which year's comments to read." This was always on the beam. The nonsmiling year was the year of the parents' divorce, the big move, the year drug use started, or some other significant event in the student's life.

The very first conference I had was with a young man named Melvin and his dad. As we went around the conference table, each teacher reported that young Melvin was failing. Since I was the drama teacher, I had the pleasure of saying that Melvin had found a niche in my class as the cameraman, and, despite his failure to turn in any homework, he was still passing with a low "D for dog."

When each adult had finished painting his or her picture of Melvin's lack of motivation and effort, the boy's father turned to his son and prepared to speak. I was thinking, *Boy, my dad would be furious with me right now. I hope this guy takes it easy on his kid in here. This is rough stuff, and, after all, he is only thirteen years old.* The father took an interesting approach. "Melvin," he said, "name one thing about each teacher that you don't like." This was not the path I would have chosen to travel, but I figured the guy had to have a point at the end of this. After all, I was a teacher, and we are helpless idealists.

Melvin responded, "I hate English class because I have to read. In history, I don't like Mr. So-and-So because we are always reading. Same thing in science. That textbook is boring. In math, she makes us do all of these word problems. In Fogelstrom's drama class, he makes us read all of these scripts."

The father looked proudly at his son for so eloquently expressing himself and then turned to us as if the argument were settled. I was perplexed. I asked Melvin, "So, the common negative factor with all of our classes is that you have to read?" He nodded. I was thinking,

Well, hell, there's *a skill he will never need. C'mon, Dad, explain the value of reading to your son!*

We all sat in silence for a few moments and then agreed to put Melvin on a weekly progress report. We would check that he had written down his homework assignments in his planner. This process helped Melvin keep organized and stay on top of exactly which assignments he was never going to turn in, no matter how many times we initialed his planner. Last I heard, when he was an adult he still did not drive because the "damn DMV makes you read a handbook and take a test to get a license." The nerve.

That year, I saw things happen in parent conferences that I never would have thought possible. One conference unveiled the father who took out a pocket knife and picked his fingernails as we spoke of his son's struggles. As he flicked dirt and skin from his nails, the others in the room struggled to stay focused. I was just happy he didn't try to cut someone.

Another conference really disturbed me. Most conferences attempt to paint a big picture, sketching in the current poor choices the child is making and then daubing in ways to correct those choices and lead the youngster into the Promised Land. We finished explaining to eighth grader Nick that he was headed the wrong way in life. After the teachers' speeches, you could have heard a pin drop in the room—we had the phenomenon lauded in Simon and Garfunkel's storied "Sound of Silence."

Then the mother turned to Nick and said, "You don't want to end up like Albert, do you?" Both started crying. That seemed to straighten Nick out.

I was thinking, *Who's Albert? What happened to Albert? Oh, man, I hope he doesn't end up like Albert. Heck, I hope I don't end up like Albert!* I have often considered using the Albert line in a conference with another family. I suppose it could work if they knew what had happened to Albert. I never did find out, though.

We had a boy named James who never made it through an entire year at a junior high without being expelled. We had a huge conference in October, just a few weeks into the year, with the principal, psychologist, and team teachers. We informed the mother that James was in peril of being ejected from our hallowed halls. Her response was, "Great. Another yearbook we paid for that we won't get!"

That was her biggest concern—not that James was failing, not that James was a discipline problem, and not that James was on his way to juvenile hall. The all-important thing was that she had paid thirty dollars for that yearbook she wouldn't get if James were expelled. We promised to mail it to her, and the conference ended.

What can get one ready for such a world? My college professor for Methods of Teaching hadn't prepared me for the cross-dressing father, the stressed-out grandma, or the auntie or uncle who showed up at a conference poised to chew us all out.

We had one girl who supposedly had a rare case of lupus, which allegedly meant she was in such constant pain that she just could not contain herself in class. This was ironic, because her favorite thing to do was to show pictures of herself water-skiing on the weekends, and her second favorite activity was to pick fights down by the minimart on the corner. One might have thought that, being afflicted by such pain, she would refrain from "whoopin' some kid's ass" for a Slurpee. *Maybe the sugar balances her system*, I hypothesized. She never got into more than one fight in a day, so perhaps my theory was correct. In any case, the important thesis was that her behavior was the disease's fault, not hers.

When we met, we decided, at the insistence of our principal, that when Erica misbehaved, we would hold up a green card as a warning. If the behavior continued, we would brandish a red card as a second warning. Ultimately, a blue card would inform Erica that she had to leave our room and go to another teacher's room, take out her sustained silent-reading book, and refocus herself.

This system made my room like the Indianapolis 500. I never knew which flag to hold out. Were we racing yet, or were we in caution mode? Had there been an accident? It was nuts. Luckily, after two days, Erica informed us that her mother told her she "didn't have to do none of this stuff," so we created a new plan that we knew she would never follow anyway.

One year later, an old friend of Erica's showed up to my class to inform me that Erica had been on television that summer. This girl said I just had to see the video, which was of a famous syndicated trashy talk show's episode entitled, "I Want to Be in a Gang." The kid achieved legendary status in one summer with all the local teens.

I had always thought those shows were staged. I mean, where would such cretins come from, right? There were Erica and her mother, screaming and yelling at the audience. The security on the show almost had to eject them, but they must not have had blue cards. (Or was it red? I never could get that right.) Erica had made a decision to buck all forms of civility and education, and we all know how powerful decisions, and especially wrong choices, can be.

After Macbeth kills King Duncan, his life's path goes through, and ultimately ends in, hell. Poor decision-making such as Macbeth's makes for wonderful class discussions. While Macbeth takes the on-ramp of the road to destruction, high school students, through poor decisions and asinine acts, sometimes put themselves on the path to Saturday School, the proverbial road not to be taken. In my pursuit of extra money to cover my daughter's year-round swim team experience, I ran the Saturday School program on campus, selling four hours of my life for a paltry wage and a pot of porridge. Voluntarily, I locked myself in a room with twenty or so "rule breakers" like the ones you saw in *The Breakfast Club*, but without the cool background music playing.

While the term *program* might imply "a rehabilitation process, with round table dialogue and therapeutic elements," the reality was much closer to the "rehabilitation" goal of our prison systems: warehouse the inmates while they do their time. For four straight hours, students sat in a classroom "reading" or "doing homework" while I graded papers at my desk. The only rules were that they couldn't sleep or "do nothing." The creativity shown by these twenty students amazed me. Many pretended to read by staring at a book but didn't turn a page for four hours, which must have caused them eye damage.

My Saturday School regulars, smiles on their faces, often greeted me during the school week with, "See you this Saturday, Mr. F.!" After running Saturday School for a few years, I decided to implement a brief discussion at the end of each session, a sort of confessional (a "shrift" moment in Shakespearean tongue) in which we'd endeavor to flesh out why the kids found themselves staring at walls in a classroom on a Saturday morning and what they could do to avoid this horrible torture in the future. This cathartic act certainly roots itself in Greek tragic theater.

In my zeal to show these students where they had "gone wrong," I opened myself up to conversations that I often regretted hearing. Still, this confessional always amused me, because, as in the prison system, repeat offenders never truly "get it." They always blame someone else for the fact that their behinds grace student desks when they could be home in bed, sleeping late.

One of the most memorable sessions went something like this:

I thumbed through the paperwork and asked, "So, Michael, why are you in here today?"

As usual, this was followed by predictable teen logic. "My vice-principal hates me! My teacher hates me! This school is hella strict!"

While vice-principals may have the time to make extensive charts of students they despise and then act on that hatred by assigning Saturday School as revenge, the more rational explanation defies this paranoid world view. "But, Michael, it says right here on the referral that in Mr. Craig's class, you were playing the 'penis game.'"

Of course, chuckles burbled around the room, and Michael, who you would think would have been embarrassed, responded, "So what? I was done with my homework."

What was I supposed to do with this juvenile court case? I, with fear and trepidation, decided to temper things smoothly despite the rough ground we were starting to march.

At times like this, a teacher has to make a split-second decision. Curious about what, exactly, the "penis game" entailed, I might easily have asked for an explanation, which Michael no doubt would have delivered in great detail with wonderful expression, but I avoided a possible lawsuit by just moving on with generalities and comments about time management and the value of working ahead in the curriculum instead of screwing around when done with work.

After looking through referrals related to truancies, tardies, and verbal altercations with teachers, I came across James's referral. "So, James, do you know why you are in here today?"

James, who had been trying to sleep without being caught, stared at me with a backward Nike logo embedded in his forehead. I suppose he had worn the Nike gloves to improve pencil grip while he was drawing stick figures and gang signs, and when he had placed his face down on his hands to rest his head, the logo must have pushed into his skin and imprinted itself. This temporary tattoo added a little extra theatrics to the moment.

Now fully awake, he replied, "Mr. Craig hates me." Another conspiracy theory, another student naming Mr. Craig, who, with the complicity of other teachers, probably had his own list of despised students whom he cannily sentenced to Saturday School. The plot had truly thickened now.

According to this typical line of student-think, there is an underground society of teachers, administrators, janitors, and cafeteria workers who, having donned dark robes, meet beneath the library to take a blood oath to ruin the lives of a select group of kids on campus each year. The parents of these students are well aware of these conspirators, and without fail blame them during parental conferences, but the rest of the campus remains ignorant of this cabal. The cursed students are then placed in Saturday School with me due to no fault of their own. Their innocence is obvious: just ask them. Macbeth had his witches to confront, and like Macbeth, these hapless victims are no match for the evil coven of teachers and administrators.

Later in life, the same curse no doubt dogs them as police officers harass them and bosses fire them "for no reason." Maybe Macbeth really was cursed, so much so that such bewitched students might relate better to him than those able to live curse-free lives outside the reach of nefarious forces. This gave me some optimism about our study of *Macbeth*.

I furthered my investigation when I saw something written on the referral that had to be cleared up before I could proclaim the innocence of James. "But, James, I see here on the referral that you were playing the 'penis game,' too. I shudder to ask, but were you playing it with Michael?"

The Saturday School crew erupted. Two boys playing the "penis game" was just too much for their immature minds. Moreover, James willingly confided that he had, indeed, been playing the "penis game" with Michael in Mr. Craig's class. Finally tired of the subject, I tried to get back to my salient point. "Well, you see what that game got you, right? Four straight hours of sitting in here on a Saturday morning. School is for learning. If you are done with your work in a class, read a book or work on something else, but do not engage in games that are named after genitalia. Now, after being stuck in here for four straight hours, I want you to think and reflect on one simple thing. Was playing 'the penis game' really worth it?"

Feeling proud of my mature, thoughtful advice, I looked to James for an appropriate response. I was determined to save this young man and put him on the road to success. He smiled and blurted, "Yeah, it was worth it, because I won."

To this day, I have no clue about the rules for playing the "penis game," but I can say without reservation that it is a game I am not entirely sure I would want to win (though I am quite confident I would not want to lose it). I am also certain that those who play it know the true meaning of Pen Island. As the Nike logo faded from the forehead, I dismissed the students and unleashed them on the world for the rest of the weekend.

Macbeth might have avoided Saturday School, but his consequences were much direr than getting up early, missing a Frosted Flakes breakfast, and being shackled for four hours in a room. After Duncan's murder, Macbeth no longer speaks to his wife about his true feelings, can't sleep because of the guilt, and continues his fall deeper into depraved acts of violence against people he once called friends. Death after death ensues, with Banquo bludgeoned and Macduff's entire family hacked up. As the play proceeds, the murders become more and more ludicrous. Duncan's demise is tragic, Banquo's is melodramatic, but the execution of Macduff's family is over-the-top silliness. Dignity disappears, and the play devolves into a circus of the absurd.

All of us become callous about behaviors in which we engage repeatedly. Macbeth opens up the opportunity to plumb with teenagers the descent into evil as we examine how, if one repeats immoral deeds again and again, it becomes easier and easier to commit each new one. I bring up the analogy of the blisters that develop on a guitar player's hands such that the player no longer feels pain, as the blisters have become calluses.

If you broach this analogy, though, be prepared for students to begin debating which guitar player is the best, whether rap is better than heavy metal or classic rock, and for at least one student each year to ask, "Can I bring my guitar in?"

Go ahead and say yes. The one time I did, it turned out to be one of the most amusing presentations on homelessness I've ever witnessed.

When we changed the senior-project specifications one year, many seniors were outraged that we had made it more "academic" in its approach. No longer could one just go rock climbing, scuba diving, or ladybug breeding and then write it up and tell about it.

My aforementioned budding Segovia had been waiting for three years to play his guitar for his senior project, so he was not to be denied. He came in and asked me point-blank, "What is the lowest possible score I can receive on the senior-project presentation and still get a C grade in this class?" This was not a common inquiry, but I computed and told him that a score of sixty out of a hundred would keep him in the grade range that his parents would find acceptable enough to allow him to have his graduation party and trip. He then asked if he could bring his guitar in early the next morning to store in my room. I approved his humble petition.

His presentation in class that day went like this:

"Hello. I am here today to talk about the homeless problem. Let me quote for you some statistics." At this point, he explained some of his research. "Now, let's break this word down."

He printed on the board:

HOME + LESS

and drew a picture of a house. "Now, here is a *home...*" He grabbed an eraser and wiped off the top third of the house. "...and now we have *less*. So, that is what the word means. Less of a house."

After this unique visual, I dropped his grade three levels due to his misunderstanding that the homeless live in houses without roofs or in dwellings missing a third of their structure. Under his definition, when my garage door broke and was removed, I had been homeless for a week. I should have applied for some federal money.

He continued, "So, I ask all of you, my fellow students, what do homeless people do all day?" There wasn't a peep, which was nice, because that is usually what happens when I ask a class a question. "I will tell you!" he continued. "They play guitars in parks!"

At this point, he threw open his guitar case, which was on the floor, plugged in his amp, and put a sign on his case that read "Will play for food or money."

"Do you all like Led Zeppelin's 'Stairway to Heaven'?" Some of his classmates started to cheer. The kid played his guitar while students threw change and pieces of candy into his case in the front of the room. He then finished his performance to thunderous applause. "Thank you all. I appreciate your support."

Thus ended the one time I told a kid he could bring in his guitar. At least the kid displayed some soul, if not an aptitude for academic success. He got the best D-minus I have ever given; plus he left with enough money to buy two taco salads, a soda, and a wonderful, half-cooked cafeteria cookie when the lunch bell rang. He might have been the smartest student I ever had.

Students will surprise you when you least expect it. My team's history teacher—we were "cored" that year—asked his students why people are not more moved by the deaths of thousands of people in modern-day Africa or by the millions during the Holocaust. One student raised his hand and replied, "Because, Mr. Kish, we only have room in our hearts for one death at a time."

Cha-ching! Easy money made in the classroom that day. Simple and profound, always the formula when high school students have something honestly worth sharing. Quotable at fourteen, and totally unaware of his profundity.

These are the moments when you can't believe you actually get paid to do the job.

I had one amazing student whose essay I always placed on the bottom of the pile, because, like dessert, I saved it for last. I just knew it was going to be something special. It was like the last birthday present that you know is going to be the topper, so you save it until the others have been opened. We were studying Helen of Troy from *The Iliad,* so I decided to read Doolittle's poem "Helen" with my students.

One ninth-grade girl described the poem's "voice" this way: "The speaker seems to be stoning Helen to death with syllables." Wow! I wish I had written that! Excellent and worthy of the bottom of the pile that evening, as it blew away the senior MLA research papers I had labored through that day.

I contrast such experiences with the mighty Martin, who did his senior project on the topic of music—not censorship in music or any other controversial issue, but...just music. His visual for his presentation was a lime-green piece of construction paper to which two pictures of instruments were affixed. The pictures, downloaded from the Internet, must have been too small, so he had enlarged them to the point where nobody could tell what the instruments were due to the pixelation.

It didn't matter, though, because Martin began to use various items in the room to make...music. He hit the desk and clapped books together, and I clearly remember him grabbing the fan in the corner, turning it on, and then singing into the blade with the fan on high speed to make his voice warble. That was it. For a scholarly MLA research paper and presentation, the mighty Martin stepped up the plate and foul tipped while trying to bunt. He hit the D-minus because the fan thing was rather creative.

We teachers must cherish the occasional brilliant minds that walk through our doors, because such students are therapy for us. Sometimes, though, students use our classes as their own therapies. During senior-project presentations one year, my lower-level English class turned into a Narcotics Anonymous meeting, a gay pride rally, and a Planned Parenthood session all in one afternoon.

One student's presentation on legalizing marijuana got about three minutes into the required ten-minute speech when he said, "I ain't gonna lie. I smoke hella weed, and it's f—d up my life. I used to like football and sports and stuff, but now I just wanna get high." I checked my assessment rubric for this segment of the speech. Not finding one, I put my pencil down when I noticed the rest of the room was fully engaged with young Billy.

Responses such as "I hear ya!" and "True dat!" flew around the class.

Billy refocused himself and finished his speech, but, strangely, he ended with the thesis that marijuana should be legalized. I asked him why he had taken that stand when he had just expressed how destructive the drug had been to his own life. He said, "If weed were legal, the cops would quit hasslin' me and my friends."

That left me sort of confused, but it did furnish me with a nice example of situational irony for future reference, though at that moment I could not believe the contradiction before me.

However, my astonishment at young Bill's logic was trumped by the next person, who presented on gay rights. Aisha stood up, announced that she was a lesbian, and before I could stop her, she displayed her PowerPoint slides that named every other lesbian she claimed was on campus. With the right to anonymity having been trampled on and a future lawsuit pending against me, I felt perhaps she should move on rapidly toward her thesis. I doubt she had any signed consent forms for "outing" her fellow classmates. At the midpoint of her speech, she then pulled out a big bag and announced it was filled with "things lesbians use" in their private lives. I stood up, thanked her for the visual, told her she was getting credit for having brought it in, but requested she go ahead and leave that bag shut for the good of the order. Much like Pandora's Box, we were saving the world by keeping it closed. Seniors can only handle so much in one afternoon.

She concluded that gay marriage should be legalized for lesbians but not for homosexual men, because that was, in her exact words, "hecka nasty." So, after the pro-marijuana dope smoker who had proclaimed that marijuana ruined his life, I had the homophobic lesbian, which nicely set the stage for my final presentation of the day, the one on teen pregnancy.

Nicky did an excellent job with her PowerPoint presentation on the economic impact of teen pregnancy, elaborating on statistics that showed how mothers in their teens struggle with a wide range of issues. I was so proud of her that I joined in her presentation by speaking about a typical day in the life of the parents of a newborn. I wrote various times of day and night on the whiteboard, itemizing each time's parental responsibilities, with an emphasis on feedings and finances. I asked the class to imagine doing all of this alone.

Many seemed shocked at what I'd said. Then I told Nicky, "I am absolutely impressed with your research. You have supported your clear, well-thought-out thesis that girls should wait to have children until they are mature and financially secure in life. Your last three months of research truly paid off. I am glad you won't have to go through many of the things you mentioned in your presentation."

She replied, "Too late."

All of the girls jumped up and said, "Oh, congratulations! I am so happy for you. When are you due?" Hugs and praises abounded. I stood there and waited for the bell that would save me from this *Alice in Wonderland* world of strange characters and twisted reason.

That day remains the nadir of dysfunction in my teaching career. When Nicky said she was going to do research on teen pregnancy, I did not know how serious she was about the topic. Somewhere in the course of reading up on birth control and teen mothers, she had put herself into the mix. Had she researched the space program, she might be orbiting the world at this very moment. I suppose the good news is that half of the class didn't pay attention to anything anyone said during the presentations, anyway.

I had several students who chose not to give their speeches, thus dooming their final grades, but who wanted to carry on social side conversations during others' presentations. How did such kids always end up sitting next to each other when my seating chart was alphabetical? Anyway, I was so fed up one year that I told two such babblers, "Hey, Corey and James, why don't you two just sit outside and do something productive instead of talking through each person's presentation?"

They looked at me angrily and said, "Yeah? Like what?"

I responded, "Perhaps now would be a good time to coordinate your carpool schedule for summer-school English through the alternative education system."

They were quiet after that. I did see them pass a few notes, but I assumed those were directions to their domiciles in preparation for English instruction in July, so I let it go.

10

THE EVERLASTING GOBSTOPPER

**Now good digestion wait on appetite,
And health on both!**
Macbeth Act III

Students begin to nod off in *Macbeth* during the conversation between Macduff and Malcolm, King Duncan's son and "hair" to the throne, to choose my students' spelling. In it, Malcolm tests Macduff's allegiance. Will he consider following a horrible ruler like Macbeth? Macduff hears Malcolm confess his own shortcomings: he suffers from greed, womanizing, and a host of other evils that will plague Scotland if he ascends to the throne. He describes himself as worse than Macbeth. Macduff, torn between the confirmedly evil Macbeth and the true heir to the throne, who appears to be a tyrant as well, concludes that Malcolm is "not fit to live."

Malcolm then reveals that he has been lying about himself to test Macduff. This scenario totally baffles students who don't understand the test itself, why there needs to be a test, or why the test is pass-fail when there is always room for extra points if a person can guess right or glance around while pretending to scratch his or her forehead.

If Macduff had a file with a 504 plan in it, he might have been able to bypass the whole cat-and-mouse game by requiring Malcolm to ask him visually and audibly if he could trust him. Maybe Macduff's mom should have sent Malcolm an e-mail contending that the test was too hard and that Macduff had been up so late playing video games that he'd been too tired to study.

What's more, Macduff's ink cartridge had gone dry just as he was printing up his homework and study guide for the test, so he would have to take the test another day—but not in the morning, because he can't get to Malcolm's on time because of ride issues, and not after school, because that is when he gets his little brother, and not during lunch, because that represents free time, and no one should be required to give up free time. Even if Macduff were to give up lunch for such a test, that is when he goes to the library to charge up his iPhone, so he cannot listen to anyone later in the day when he slips his headphones on in class.

Kids love to hide their earbuds in their clothes with the wire up through the necks of their shirts. It looks like the Secret Service in my room. Half of the time, I am waiting for the POTUS to come through my door. I am convinced that the long hair many young men are wearing these days is a direct result of their desire to listen surreptitiously to iPods during class. Ultimately, Malcolm's test of Macduff seems quite unfair, because, after all, it *was* a test, and tests just aren't very nice.

My colleague once told me that he uses *Willy Wonka and the Chocolate Factory* to teach this concept. I tried it one year: "Well, guys, it is like the scene in *Willy Wonka*." The entire room lit up like a Christmas tree.

A hand shot to the sky. "You mean the Johnny Depp one?"

The girls began to talk about how sometimes he looks good but can also be a bit weird in other movies. Most of the girls were now dreaming about Johnny Depp. Meanwhile, most of the guys were thinking about chocolate. "No, not the Johnny Depp one. The older one with Gene Wilder."

Blank faces greeted the Gene Wilder explanation. "OK, it's the one you saw when you were little. There are only two versions, and since it is not Johnny Depp's, we all know which one I'm talking about, right?" Most nodded accordingly. "Now, in the old one…"

A hand shot up.

"Yes?"

"Was that old one in color?"

"Yes. At least, I have always seen it in color. Are we good now? All right, in the old one, there is a scene where Charlie Bucket gives…"

Another hand.

"You know, I heard that they can color movies and stuff. So maybe that one was actually in black and white, and then they added the color later."

Someone else announced, "When I was little, I thought that there was a time when the world was in black and white because of old pictures and movies. Now I know that isn't true, or at least I think it might not be true. I think my big brother lied to me."

I desperately tried to get us back to the point I was making. "Yes, they do colorize movies, but I think that one was in color originally. The point is, when Charlie Bucket has the everlasting gobstopper, he then decides to…yes?"

"Do they sell those?"

"What?"

"Everlasting gobstoppers."

"I don't think they sell any candy that lasts forever. But regular gobstoppers are real."

A normally quiet student raised his hand and proclaimed, "I heard that tire companies have created a rubber that won't break down, but they don't use it because they want people to keep buying tires."

Another brain sparked to life at this revelation and spewed forth, "I heard there are aliens in New Mexico. I saw it on the History Channel."

General comments of "for real?" and "tires are hella expensive" bounced off the walls, but not a whisper in the general direction of the discussion about the play or the issue at hand. "Ummm, I think that we are moving away from why I brought Willy Wonka up. Listen, Charlie Bucket gives the everlasting gobstopper back to Willy Wonka in the end, and then Willy Wonka...yes?"

"You just said there was no such thing as an everlasting gobstopper!"

"There isn't in real life, but we are talking about a movie here, remember? Now, Charlie Bucket gives the item back to Willy Wonka, and then Willy Wonka rewards Charlie by giving him the factory. Willy Wonka acted rudely toward Charlie to test him and see if Charlie would sell the gobstopper to the competitor behind Wonka's back, and Charlie passed the test by giving Wonka the candy back. He won. That is what Macduff does. He passes the test. He gives the metaphoric gobstopper back to Malcolm when he says he would never follow an evil ruler. Got it?"

A kid in the back chuckled to himself, "Bucket...hella dumb last name."

Before I could address this slander against poor Charlie Bucket, another student asked, "Do they sell those?"

"They do not sell everlasting gobstoppers, if that is what you asking me. We covered that already."

"I heard that. I'm not deaf, you know. I just want to know if they sell metaphoric gobstoppers. I think I saw some of those at Safeway."

I replied thoughtfully, "I think they do, too. They are right next to the Excedrin migraine medicine. I will check for you today after school when I hit aisle two."

The play moves on toward its bloody end as several prophecies given to Macbeth make him feel secure. He is told that he will remain king until the woods get up and walk to the castle and that no man "born of woman" can kill him. This would make anyone feel secure, but by now, the students should have down the irony of the witches and their equivocation. If a teacher keeps questioning students about a few literary terms repeatedly during the study of a piece of literature, eventually they will get it.

Of course, all teachers learn that constant questioning is the Socratic method of instruction. The assumption is that we all have knowledge within our minds and that a skillful questioner can extract it. I once mentioned the Socratic method to my seniors and gave them the definition found in a literary terms dictionary: "a systematic method of doubt to elicit an implicit truth." When I explained the phrase, students just did not get the meaning from the definition we were told to give them.

The emphasis on such terms as *Socratic method* came from the desire of our superintendent that year that every grade level teach "100 Facts" that students would memorize. Each English grade level scrambled for literary terms, and we arm-wrestled other grade levels for dominance. Somehow, we were lucky enough to get *Socratic method* on our list. Within two years, our superintendent was gone, and the "100 Facts" went with him. But it was a glorious two years. I love changing visions and standards constantly.

After fighting through the definition for a few minutes, I watched a student walk in tardy. I told her to stand right there at the threshold. I then informed the class that I would show them how the Socratic method worked. "Ashley, why are you tardy?"

Ashley, totally embarrassed, had no clue that the other thirty-plus students had been learning about the Socratic method. She just wanted to slide into her seat unnoticed, but now that option was long gone. "I got up late," she mumbled.

"Why?"

"Because I was tired."

Beginning to sort of enjoy this, I asked, "Why?"

"Because I went to bed late."

"Why?" The class now began to see where this was headed and chuckled.

"Because I was talking on the phone late last night with my friend."

"Why?"

"Because my friends are important to me," she spouted. Ashley seemed to be getting irritated.

"Why?"

"Huh?"

"Why are your friends important to you?"

"I don't know. I guess I don't want to be a loner. I don't want to be by myself."

"Eureka! You can sit down now, Ashley. Class, we all now know a truth about Ashley purely as the result of a system of doubt. She has just told us that she does not want to be by herself in life and that her friends are critical to her well-being. Chalk one up for Socrates."

To this day, I doubt Ashley has a clue about why I questioned her that morning. However, the example worked perfectly for every other student in the room. Maybe the Greeks did know what they were talking about.

Of course, the names of the Greeks and their gods always confuse the kids if you get beyond the Disney version of Hercules. I once had a student mention the Greek god Herpes on a test, but that was OK because Herpes's companion was Chlamydia, the flaming hero of justice. I love teaching the Greeks.

After seeing the light on the various issues related to Willy Wonka, the everlasting gobstopper, and Malcolm's test of Macduff, students eagerly anticipate finding out whether Macduff passes the test. After Malcolm's acknowledgment that he would make an evil ruler, Macduff responds that such a person is "not fit to live" and laments, "O Scotland!" Macduff will never join anyone evil and Malcolm's lie about his true nature reveals Macduff's real one.

At that point, I typically state, "Bingo! He just handed back the everlasting gobstopper. He passed the test. Malcolm now gives him the factory metaphorically as he announces he will be a king who is commanded by his country and delights 'no less in truth than in life.'" Of course, the class just sits there, mouths agape, perplexed that I have mixed chocolate with gobstoppers and tests with Scottish factories and monarchs. So, I then break it down to its simplest form and announce, "Macduff passed the test! Malcolm will be a great king! Can anyone speculate as to why Malcolm tested Macduff in this way?"

Crickets...

No one ever figures it out. I would even welcome a wrong attempt at that question.

I had an autistic student years ago who endeared himself to me by consistently answering questions wrong, but always with the same answer. He became fixated on certain things in class. Dominic always raised his hand enthusiastically when I quizzed the class on comprehension (or, as theorists put it, I checked for meaning).

I found out what Dominic was thinking about while I taught each day, which explained his beatific smile. His answer? When I called on him, 90 percent of the time, I'd hear, "A beautiful woman!" While I am not quite sure this answer is ever off target, it did become amusing that Dominic thought this the answer to almost every question.

I decided to rig the class for Dominic's success one afternoon. I found a sonnet by Edmund Spenser and asked the class, "So, what is this poem about?" When Dominic repeated his time-tested answer, I announced to the class that he was indeed correct in his analysis. To further develop Dominic's self-esteem, I read from some of Byron's works. I asked, "What is this one about, Dominic?" Bang. Same answer. His smile almost cracked his cheeks. It was his shining moment. It was the day "a beautiful woman" held greater meaning than ever before and was always the correct answer to any question posed.

Dominic also had a strange habit of counting down the last ten seconds of the period in a booming voice. I could not break him of it. The first time he did it, I about wet myself. I was closing out my first-day-of-school lesson and a bit on edge, as most teachers are on day one of the year, and as I was saying, "For homework, you all need to get your management plans signed, and…"

"*Ten! Nine! Eight! Seven! Six…*" He was staring at his watch intently, and when he hit "*One!*" the bell sounded. He looked up to the heavens and said, "Booya!"

I was stunned. This sequence happened every single school day of the year. I was powerless to stop it. The rocket was launching, and I had to get on it or get out of the way, so I jumped on and let Dominic signal the end of each third period. Right in the middle of something significant, I'd announce, "I'd better hurry, because the countdown is coming." The kids grew to like it, and so did I. Dominic meant no harm and was quite proud of his ability to coordinate his watch exactly with the school clocks.

One time when the bells did not ring correctly, he kept muttering to himself, "Incorrect! Incorrect! Incorrect!"

To which I replied, "Hey, Dominic, remember…a beautiful woman." He smiled and let go of the time fiasco that day.

I have often wondered what job Dominic has secured in adulthood. Does he coordinate the entrances and exits of runway models for posh high-fashion shows? Such a job would blend his two favorite things. Either that, or he works for *New Year's Rockin' Eve* in the winter and NASA for the remainder of the year. Yearly at midnight, I strain to pick out his voice over the cacophony of the Times Square crowd with his patented countdown developed in my English class. If you listen carefully, you might hear "Booya!" when the crystal ball signals the coming of the New Year to the Square. Try it this year and let me know. Though adult Dominic might be working for NASA now on their rocket-launch sequence, even Dominic as a beauty obsessed teenager would have a hard time defining Lady Macbeth as "a beautiful woman" in light of her true character.

Act V lays bare for all to see that Lady Macbeth's mind is ravaged by guilt. Her sleepwalking scene is a masterpiece of psychological insight. Do not show the Polanski film version, though, because Lady Macbeth, candlestick in hand, walks around the room au naturel. This is not surprising, given that the film was produced by Playboy.

Each year when the film begins and the kids see Hugh Hefner's name in the credits, all the guys perk up until they hear the Elizabethan English spoken by the characters in the film. The witch with no eyes freaks them out, which deletes anything related to Playboy from their minds: you know they hate Shakespeare when a naked woman speaking Elizabethan English is boring to them.

Dominic would have loved it. If he had been alive when the Polanski version was produced, I would have looked for his name in the credits. I do hear bells in the film, though, and there might even be a countdown if you listen hard enough.

You know, I might be on to something.

11

SPOTS, WALKING TREES, C-SECTIONS, AND SPIDERMAN

Is't night's predominance, or the day's shame,
That darkness does the face of earth entomb,
When living light should kiss it?
Macbeth Act II

Lady Macbeth wanders the castle each night in her sleep and mutters lines that forever have been used as jokes by English teachers and satirists. Her most famous line comes when she is rubbing her hands while attempting to cleanse herself of the evil murder and says, "Out, damned spot!" Of course, the joke about her kicking a dog out of the castle is so old as to not even be funny anymore, but I reference it anyway with the kids. Amazingly, no one falls for the "there is a dog in the castle" trick anymore.

They do fall for a pet trick, though, in *To Kill a Mockingbird*, so if you are teaching that book, you can enjoy the scene where Atticus Finch kills the rabid dog. The dog's name is Tim Johnson. Students rush in every year after reading that chapter for homework and say, "I cannot believe Atticus killed that guy!" Many students think good old Tim was a drunk man staggering his way down the street. I suppose the dog might have been inebriated rather than rabid, and Atticus had to shoot him before he did something horrible.

While I do understand the awkwardness of a dog named Tim Johnson, apparently many people in the southern part of the United States name their pets with first and last names. I only discovered this by accident in the teacher lunchroom one day. A lady who used to live in Texas was talking about Lucky Kingsford's diet issues. I asked her if that was really the person's name, and she said it was her cat. Enlightened to the pet-naming proclivities of Texans, I now knew why the dog Tim had a last name. Still, if you can name a dog whatever name you want, pick something unique, like "Zeus."

I had a squirrel that used to come and sit outside my classroom a few years ago. The kids named him Euripides. It made me proud that they would find such a great way to honor a Greek dramatist. He was there every day after lunch, eating garbage by a tree. A student would yell, "Mr. Fogie, Euripides is back!" and we all would look out the window. I changed rooms the next year. I miss that little guy. By the way, do the Greeks have last names? Socrates, Plato, Euripides, Sophocles, Homer? The list goes on. Maybe just their pets had last names? Someone should do a doctoral Dissertation on why we refer to Greeks by just a single name. I would read it.

The animal-school connection is hardly new. When I was in high school, I remember sitting in a portable out on the blacktop for my Spanish class. Two kids were whispering during a test. Their subdued words were in English, so I knew they were not cheating. They were saying something like, "Yup, here they come," and "It is working," and "Any minute now."

Thoroughly confused, I looked at them, and they nodded toward the open portable door. On the stairway that led up to the classroom, they had placed a trail of bologna. About a hundred seagulls were circling the portable, and one had made its way right up to the door opening and was now walking into the room. If this had been an English class, I fear that the teacher would have had to deal with the symbolism of a swarm of gulls circling overhead with full stomachs. If that is not a sign to find a new job, then my analysis of literature is quite off.

Speaking of symbolism, Lady Macbeth constantly seeks to have light near her. This obviously contrasts with her earlier evil prayer for darkness to engulf Inverness, as well as representing her separation from all that is good and holy. She seeks a light, a spiritual peace, even if it is somewhat counterfeit. Meanwhile, her husband sits in an ostensibly secure state falsely created by the witches who have told him that "none born of woman" can harm him and that he will remain king until "Birnam Wood come to Dunsinane." Since there are no test-tube babies around in Scotland and this is not the *Lord of the Rings* with walking trees, it appears that Macbeth will reign for a long time.

The long journey is now coming to an end, you are in Act V, and you have become Lightning McQueen at the end of the movie *Cars*. It is time to push the other car across the finish line to thunderous applause because, quite frankly, the kids are out of gas.

As Malcolm marches toward the final confrontation with Macbeth, his men "hew" down some "boughs." Of course, few students actually hew much in their lives and probably don't have to mess with many boughs, either. You can try to help them by singing, "When the *bough* breaks, the cradle will fall, and down will come baby, cradle, and all" to put the vocabulary word in context. One year, this initiated a nice discussion about how twisted and horrible that little song is and that the fact that someone would put their baby in a tree is probably a cry for help. The song also put many in a state of confusion: on the final test, when I asked them why the "bough" line from the play was significant, at least three students wrote about the baby in the tree who was not "born of woman." Once again, the lint roller picked up a bit here and a bit there.

At least by the end, they know that Malcolm's men are carrying tree branches to hide their numbers as they approach Macbeth's lair. The forest has come to Macbeth, his security begins to fade, and the bloody conclusion is coming. Macbeth receives word that his wife has died. His speech appropriately sums up his life when he says, "Tomorrow and tomorrow and tomorrow creeps in this petty pace from day to day to the last syllable of recorded time…Out, out, brief candle! Life's but a walking shadow, a poor player who struts and frets his hour upon the stage and then is heard no more. It is a tale told by an idiot…" At this point, be thankful that you do not have ninth graders. Anytime a curse word appears in any written work or film, they all go "Oooooooooo," and then look at you. This is truly ironic, because you can follow the nicest kid out of class and hear him or her drop a dozen swear words, but a word like *idiot* will cause students to react as if their ears were melting.

When I taught eighth grade and they read *The Call of the Wild*, the school mandated that we play an audio version for them. That was a true nightmare. In theory, the students were supposed to follow the book while the audio played. I battled for about four days to make sure they were following along, but it became exhausting. Toward the end, many would put their heads down and just listen. After two years of this, I started to wait for the one line in the book that would wake them all up. The audio would be humming along to the sounds of slumber, and the line would come: "No, sir. You can go to hell, sir." Thirty-five heads would pop up like they had been shocked by a Taser, giggle for five seconds, and then drop right back down. I vowed that year to never play an audiobook again unless *The Catcher in the Rye* is the title being taught. I would rather make them read aloud or listen to my own voice. I was bored out of my mind on those days.

One year, I had student named Jamal who fell asleep during the recording. The last minute of the period, he was still asleep, so I told the class to quietly leave, and we would shut the lights off for him. Eighth-grade students love this type of stuff. The kids tiptoed out of the room like Santa's little helpers on Christmas Eve, and the lights were dimmed in preparation for the theatrics about to begin. The bell rang, and we all walked around the outside of the building to my classroom's window. We hit the window one time hard and watched the fun.

It was a cloudy day, so no light went into the room from outside. The clock never worked in there, so no one knew what time it was without a watch, and unfortunately for Jamal, this occurred during the days before cell phones, and he was not wearing a timepiece. He woke up and panicked. Apparently, he thought it was late into the night. He grabbed his backpack and sprinted out of the classroom and down the hall. He probably thought he was going to miss the bus or perhaps his dinner. He came back the next day and laughed about it. Oh, he never fell asleep again in class, either. Lesson learned.

In his waning moments, Macbeth is left with one final shred of hope: no man born of woman can harm him. Of course, he also knows that since people carrying sticks can count for a forest uprooting itself, he is pretty much doomed. Macduff has pursued his revenge and proclaims loudly to Macbeth that he was "untimely ripped from his mother's womb." This will confuse most of the class, so a discussion will ensue about cesarean births. Be prepared for conversations about birthing videos, YouTube, and some personal tales from students about the day they entered the world. My personal favorite was the one where the student's mother went into labor after riding a roller coaster at an amusement park. Apparently, those warning signs are tough to read. Her son pretty much ignored directions on assignments, so perhaps it was genetic. While most students will understand the physiology of this last "prophecy" and the equivocation behind it, some students aren't "worldly" enough yet to get it. That can be a major problem at times in high school.

A student of mine, a young, sophomore girl to be exact, was presenting her research findings during the teaching of *Frankenstein*. Her group was discussing the creation of artificial life as well as the idea of cloning and the use of stem cells. Their job was to connect these modern issues to the novel in some way. This student was the nicest girl in the world. She beamed innocence and purity. As she was presenting, she kept using the wrong word for *organism*. There she was, in front of a class filled with mostly juniors and seniors, smiling and enthusiastically proclaiming the modern marvels of the artificial *orgasm*. In the back of the room, a few senior girls were really starting to crack up, but quietly, so you could see their minds seeping out into the sides of their mouths and cheeks. You could read their faces as they twitched and shook and looked at each other. This is when you really have to watch yourself as a teacher. I did not want to embarrass the young lady, so I prayed that it was a slipup she would not make again. Thank goodness the seats were filled with females for this advanced class. Had this been a male-dominated course, getting the kids focused again would never have been possible.

After the third time, I made a vow to stop it if this student threw out another *orgasm*. Of course, things went smoothly until she ended with the line, "Victor Frankenstein connects with this topic because he wanted to create an *orgasm* with his bare hands." I actually wished someone would have said that when I was in high school, because that would have been the most hilarious moment of my teen years and one of those memories that people discuss at reunions. I then said, "Ummmm, Susan, I believe the word you're trying to say is *organism*." She kept smiling at me, but you could see that her brain was working overtime to comprehend what she had been saying. Once she worked out how that word would sound without the "ni" in it, she then turned bright red. I just started clapping for her group, and thunderous applause echoed from the class. She escaped with minimal social damage, and the students now have their favorite moment of high school for future discussion at parties, bar mitzvahs, and weddings.

You are now within moments of completing the reading of a tragic play by the greatest writer of all time. You are but a page turn away from signing off. Students are aware of this anyway, because they always turn the pages in the textbook to see how much reading is left. Watch the pages turn anytime you start reading something with them and announce, "Now, finish this short story on your own." Ninety percent of the kids in the room will research exactly how much of it is left, and if it is over two pages, they will moan and groan, and many students will roll their eyes in disgust.

When Macbeth gets his head cut off, you know the man has been given his "comeuppance," so to speak. Powerful lessons about greed and blind ambition are absorbed through the dialogue and action. In the theater, the applause will sound, heads will nod with approval, and a sense of closure will envelope the audience. It remains profound after centuries in performance. Mel Brooks once said, "It's good to be the king!" After this play, we all wonder, *Is it?* This is why I spend several months covering the monarchy as we build toward the end of the play. Students need to be aware of what various kings go through: family squabbles, the necessity of a male heir, and the incredible pressure involved in being the sovereign. When I ask former students what they remember about this unit, most smile and state that Henry VIII's armor was "hella funny." There it is. After weeks and weeks of detailed information and intrigue about politics, leadership, philosophy, and religion, students remember a twenty-second picture of Henry VIII's armor with his massive codpiece sticking out from the crotch and the fact that he was fifty-four inches around the girth.

With this in mind, I realize that finishing this play with high school kids is quite a different matter from the feeling in a theater as the tragedy closes. The final lines of the play read: "So thanks to all at once and to each one, whom we invite to see us crowned at Scone." Malcolm uses the plural pronoun for himself, which reveals he is now speaking like the reigning monarch. Students miss that change in diction and wonder why several people are being crowned at a delicious piece of quick bread that can be dipped in their mocha. So many questions: is it a pumpkin-spice scone? Lemon flavored? Cream flavored? After five acts and a dozen hours of reading and lecture, they still are baffled with its final words. It is a fine mystery. Lady Macbeth has committed suicide, her husband's head is displayed for all to see, and the focus remains on a tasty treat where someone is getting a crown. How unsatisfying to the purists, yet wonderful to the class right before lunch.

I believe I have found a better ending to the play. I cannot take credit for it, though. I had a student named Clifford who inspired my alternative ending of *Macbeth*. Of course, being named after a big, red dog was bad enough, but he chose to go by a different name: "Cliffy." Cliffy would show up to my room each morning at least an hour before the start of school. It mattered not that I was grading essays, projects, or in the middle of typing a lesson; Cliffy would sit down near my desk and proceed to tell me about his asthma, eczema, and irritable bowel syndrome. While all three of these conditions certainly are fodder for wonderful conversation and a splendid jump start to the workday, I just had a hard time focusing on his ailments as the sun rose over my room. His mother would weekly e-mail me with updates on his self-esteem and physical condition.

I had high hopes that Cliffy, as a senior, would soon shatter the shackles of his name as well as his rashes and grow up ready for the adult world. If he could have called himself "Cliff," perhaps this would have completely changed the tone around him. It made for a nice English lesson on tone and diction, but not when he was in your class. I will have to wait at least a decade until family members are out of the school district before I use his name as an example; however, when he presented his *Frankenstein* project, my hopes were strengthened momentarily that *Cliffy* would evolve into a bold adult named *Cliff*.

Cliffy created an incredible presentation that highlighted many scientific developments within the last thirty years: cloning, stem cell research, face transplantation, and robotics. He connected each and every one of these things to some segment of the novel. He had textual support, MLA documentation, pictures, graphs, embedded video clips, and just about anything you could ever ask for. The entire class did not blink as he spoke. He was articulate and organized. I sat there in awe and felt that Cliffy had turned a corner in his life. With just three weeks to go before graduation, the man was looking like a presenter for Microsoft up there. Cliffy had become Cliff. And then it happened.

He wrapped up his presentation with this exact line: "So, remember, everyone; like Spiderman says, 'With great power comes great responsibility.'" This eighteen-year-old senior was quoting a comic-book hero. He had risen out of the muck and mire only to start sinking right back down. Giggles were heard throughout the room, which is something quite foreign to a senior English class. I still felt that Cliffy had taken a step forward, though, but now I could sense the "y" creeping back into his name. And then it happened again.

Right after the quoting of Spiderman, his cell phone rang. His ring tone was the SpongeBob SquarePants cartoon theme. I wanted to run up there and save this kid, but thankfully, Cliffy's resilience and naïve approach to teen life kept him "embarrassment free" in such moments. As required by the school, I had to confiscate his phone. As he looked at the caller's ID number on his cell, he shouted, "Damn you, Mother!"

For a brief and shining moment, *Cliffy* had been *Cliff,* but now he was back in teenage wasteland. The twenty-fifth letter of the alphabet became welded to the root part of his name as he cursed his mother. With the presentation a fading memory in all of our minds, the phrase "Damn you, Mother!" on the heels of a cartoon-themed ring tone became his defining moment.

Now, taking that special experience from a high school classroom and playing around with its various interpretations, we can imagine how exciting the end of *Macbeth* would be if Cliffy had written it. Macbeth in his final moments of life, standing before Macduff, could have cried out, "With great power comes great responsibility!" Every teenager would get this point. Macbeth had failed this test and had allowed the power to corrupt him. Then, with his last breath, Macbeth could mutter these words to close the play: "Damn you, Mother!" How perfect would that be? Scholars throughout the world would wrestle with the question of what Macbeth's childhood had been like and what had led to his destruction. Was his mother just like the woman he chose as his wife in terms of dominance?

Perhaps, long ago, Macbeth went by the name of *Macbethy*. Like Cliffy, *Macbethy* was immune to the opinions of others, comfortable in his own skin, and totally naïve of the world's harsh side. Content to live as one of Scotland's nobles, *Macbethy* would have lived out his days feasting with the rest of the thanes and discussing his ailments with the local Scottish priest at the kirk. At some point in his life, Macbethy dropped the "y," and the rest is history. I advise parents to put the "y" on every single kid's name and live with the hope that genuine goodness will prevail in society. We would all have a cartoon theme running through our heads as we dealt with the troubles of the day and ambition, power, and reputation would mean zero to us.

Shakespeare may have given us the greatest works of literature, but I want to thank Cliffy for showing the entire world the nicest letter in the alphabet. Now I know why the little girl in eighth grade did not want to make the word *jury* plural. She knew the value of keeping the "y" around. I need to find that girl and apologize. If I ever see her, I will buy her a scone.

12

TO DREAM THE IMPOSSIBLE DREAM

But I remember now
I am in this earthly world, where to do harm
Is often laudable, to do good sometimes
Accounted dangerous folly;
Macbeth Act IV

The Macbeth duo had to be dreamers if they imagined they would get away with the botched and gory slaughter on that bloody night. We teachers, too, dream, but not in the same way. No realist teacher would survive the grinder of the American school day.

Most teachers incarnate the protagonist in the *Man of La Mancha* musical set in Andalusia, Spain, where the rain stays mainly on the plain. We tilt at our own windmills, deaf to the appeals of any Sancho to come to our senses by looking with the eyes of realism at the world around us. Oblivious, we sing, "To dream the impossible dream, to fight the unbeatable foe…to try when your arms are too weary…" We see each student, initially at least, as a potential "next big thing," who, influenced by our guidance, will wow the world with something that will revolutionize life for the better. We are true believers that the pursuit of happiness depends on the "fulfillment" of each student's destiny, whatever that means.

Over the years, movies have been made about teacher types, but no cinematic effort thus far has been able to capture the full breadth of our profession. Some flicks, such as *Blackboard Jungle*, *Goodbye, Mr. Chips*, and *Dead Poets' Society*, have done a good job. The trouble with all teacher movies, though, is that a film runs a story by in about two hours, whereas real teaching is done day by day for years. This means that teacher-film screenwriters usually cave to depicting a sudden transformation in students as if magic were involved. A class of disparate gang members and their hangers-on morph overnight into a tight-knit group committed not only to going to college but to an internal philosophy of support, even in such wonderful movies as *Stand and Deliver* and *Dangerous Minds*.

Changes in students are rarely as they appear in so many film depictions, but we Americans are pretty hung up on miracles. Many fancy that if we could develop the right elixir, education could leap to an astral plane of cooperation and achievement. Discussion of contemporary educational research frequently imagines a future when nutritional supplements and medications now being tested on mice will spawn a race of Nietzsche's *Übermenschen* who will learn at a rate we can barely imagine today. That's why the *National Enquirer* sells so well at grocery-store checkout stands. Do you believe in magic, too?

Myself, I preferred to anchor my teaching on the model that Winston Churchill championed when he proclaimed of the British in 1940 when they faced imminent invasion by Hitler's Germany, "We shall fight on the beaches, we shall fight on the landing grounds, we shall fight in the fields and in the streets, we shall fight in the hills; we shall never surrender." According to this "bulldog" view, a teacher bites onto students and refuses doggedly to let go, no matter what.

Teen students are notoriously inconstant. They spit on your shadow one day, and the next they act like you're their BFF—best friend forever. Usually, it's not you that changes, though even teachers have some degree of variability. Like dogs, we take the hits and the occasional strokes but remain faithful to our grand adventure: the windmills of ignorance are a foe to be overcome by our perseverance and courage. True romantics like old Alonso Quijano in his knight-errant costume, most teachers joust daily with the reality before them, refusing to accept it for what it is.

We teachers are real people, but at times, pretty odd ones. Because we spend so much time with youngsters, we learn as much from them as they do from us and even take on some of their behaviors. You'll hear us using the latest slang, unaware that it sounds as odd coming out of our adult mouths as "bitchin'" and "psych" did when they were used by our own teachers back in the day. My wife looks at me askance anytime I voice something teen current, such as, "That is so ratchet!"

Worse, though, is our unconsciously ironic failure to obey our own rules. Go to any faculty meeting, and you'll notice the same objectionable behaviors characteristic of any classroom. There are staff members such as myself who always head for the back row, where we carry on side conversations and commentary designed to entertain our section of the room. Information babbled by any principal must nearly always be repeated, because someone in the crowd will inevitably ask, "What are we supposed to do?" It's an annoyance about which we berate students regularly. Yes, we're hypocrites.

Teachers deserve amnesty for these peccadilloes, though, in that nearly everything raised in any faculty meeting could have been covered more time-efficiently in a memo. This was not so true early in my career, when we often discussed matters of real educational significance such as class size, supervisory duties, and the sharing of teaching techniques—the tools of our trade. The longer I taught, though, the greater the proportion of meeting times was devoted to "cover your ass" (CYA in military slang) folderol so that administrators could certify that they had, in fact, informed the faculty and so were absolved of responsibility later when anything went wrong.

I knew and worked closely with a host of colleagues over my career and could elaborate on dozens of them, but brevity being the soul of wit, like Polonius in *Hamlet*, I'll be brief. I will focus my thoughts on three types of teachers I've known: *tellers*, *hide-and-seekers*, and *sellers*. These three define the majority of instructors students will encounter in their school careers.

The *tellers* are those teachers who talk all period long. They don't engage students; they just talk the entire time. The *tellers* talk, most of them, for two very distinct reasons. First, if they talk all period, there is absolutely no chance of assigning any work that will be done and turned in during said instructional time, which in turn means that no papers come in to be graded. Also, some teachers just love to hear themselves, even if that means a full hour of talking about almost nothing. These teachers dominate the stage the entire time but refuse any input from students whatsoever. You will not hear the kids' voices in these classes, ever, but you will hear the groans.

The next type of teacher is the *hide-and-seeker*. These teachers, probably out of fear of speaking with students, list the assignment on the board, page numbers and all, and subsequently sit at their desks answering e-mails, playing solitaire on the computer, or checking their retirement balances online. Students, well trained, walk in, check the board, and get to work. Usually, partner work, also known as copying, is just fine in these rooms. Students finish their assignments, put them in a basket labeled "turn in" at some point, and then proceed to play with their phones, listen to music, sleep, or talk with their friends. In this room, you will hear nothing but student voices, but rarely will those voices speak much of anything related to the curriculum.

Last, the *seller* is the teacher who is in the job because he or she wants students to learn something and think along the way. The teacher will "sell" the class on an idea, get it to go to work on it, come back and use lecture if necessary to clarify things, and then turn the students loose again to figure the rest out. *Sellers* are not afraid of students in the slightest but do not want to dominate the stage; however, they will do so momentarily if instruction calls for it. These are the teachers who are exhausted at the end of the day, because selling anything takes a massive amount of energy and passion.

In the business world, these are your salesmen and saleswomen who work hard to push a product. In education, the product is an education, and the price is just hard work. But that price is expensive for some students, as their hard work "accounts" have limited funds, so negotiating takes place as the *seller* explains the importance of the assignment for a student's final grade, the relevancy of the material as a foundation for college level work, or just life in general as a form of cultural literacy.

If I could spend a day with young teachers or with students in college considering the teaching profession, I would tell them to be *sellers* when they walk into the classroom. Anything else is a disservice to students and the profession in general.

13

THE PETER PRINCIPAL: YOUR "PAL"

Within this hour at most
I will advise you where to plant yourselves,
Acquaint you with the perfect spy o' the time,
The moment on't; for't must be done tonight...
Macbeth Act III

The issue of training for leadership and hereditary succession is a prominent factor in the *Macbeth* story. How could King Duncan ensure that his son Malcolm would get the crown? His own failure to survive the Macbeths' plot left Duncan's sons as suspects in his murder. Fearing such an accusation and their own assassinations, Malcolm and Donalbain split, the former for England, the latter for Ireland.

In like manner, the question of administrative succession in American schools is a frequent source of entertainment and dismay for classroom teachers. You see, the "Peter Principle" is so engrained in the American educational fabric that one might wonder if it was named for an actual principal somewhere named Peter. It is a hackneyed observation that many school administrators "rise" from the teaching pool mainly because of their ineptitude in the classroom. The sad thing is that this is a promotion:

it almost always gets them more flexibility with their time, better work stations, and more money.

Ironically, though, some good teachers who take administrative positions end up frustrated because they have no training as leaders of adults. Their real talent is in the classroom. The few I've seen try to maintain even a skeletal teaching schedule for themselves soon find that they are so frequently pulled from their treasured teaching periods for some meeting or other that they surrender to full-time administrative duties that consign them to minimal contact with students and other teachers.

Visit a district office or county office of education, and instantly you notice the contrast between the world of teachers and the world of off-campus administrators. The clocks all tell the appropriate time, the garbage cans have plastic liners, and the water coolers are fully stocked and refreshing.

Several times in my teaching career, I have been admitted to these hallowed halls, only to experience something akin to sneaking into China's ancient Forbidden City when it was run by sheltered emperors in gilded chairs. Duncan's ironic words as he enters Inverness come to mind: "The castle hath a pleasant seat, the air numbly and sweetly recommends itself unto our gentle senses." When one gets into the educational palace, the air truly is sweet, even if things are possibly being poisoned outside.

During one enlightening episode, I sat down at the district office to work with colleagues from other schools through a common assessment for senior English. We analyzed data and developed pacing guides. These tasks, arduous in previous attempts on campus, morphed into something gloriously relaxing in the atmosphere at the DO. Bagels sat on the table in front of us, replete with cream cheese, butter, and honey. People chatted quietly in the hallways. No bells clanged on the hour. In the blessed silence, I actually heard the coffee pot brewing, and I did not hear one swear word the entire day. The computers hummed along with no keys missing. The Internet was lightning fast due to its latest browser updates and operating systems, and my seat was cushioned in the well-lit room. I thought, *Is this what the rest of the adult world experiences on a daily basis?*

I charged into my task, analyzed data, and rewrote test question after test question, but the entire time, I felt that I was cheating the state of California that day by getting paid for it. While it was not exactly Marie Antoinette decreeing, "Let them eat cake," a district higher-up came in and proclaimed near the noon hour, "We're having pizza." I'm not sure where the funds for it came from, but it was delicious.

Duncan, functioning in the placidity of his own district office, became naïve and oblivious to the plotting and scheming around him. This softening of perspective happens frequently to those who abandon the classroom for "higher ground." While I do not envy the administrators on campus who are stuck in middle management, I give little credence to the words of those who close their office doors for years as they pore over books on the latest, greatest theories about how to revolutionize learning and instruction.

The greatest irony of all is that the majority of those who hold educational doctorates will tell you why you need to "individualize" your teaching, yet if you walked into their classes at a university campus, you would see them implementing but one mode of it. They demand that students adjust to their lecture teaching style. Period. They are not subject to their own mandates, just as administrators and federal Department of Education employees do not suffer the consequences of their unfunded mandates or latest, greatest implementations. Live with your decision on a daily basis, and my ears will be open to your suggestions.

Every decade or so, the general mantra changes from the federal level on down to the state and then into your local schools. Years ago, California followed a study called *Second to None*, which called for all schools to rethink, yet again, the way they did high school. Of course, once we kind of figured out how the study should form our teaching and scheduling and content, we were then told it was time to shift to No Child Left Behind. In an ironic twist of fate, the next movement was called Race to the Top, which meant we were going to leave a child behind somewhere. After all, it's a race, for goodness' sake. But in reality, what they wanted was more like "push to the top" so that "no child would be left behind" and every kid's self-esteem would make them feel like they were "second to none" in the end.

Now with Common Core, little really is "common" to students getting hit midstream in their learning careers with new ways to do things, especially in math, and what was once "core" in English, namely expository writing based on archetypal, classical literature, is hardly recognizable anymore as students read editorials and massive amounts of non-fiction. All worthy pursuits, but hardly core, or common, to education over the centuries. Harold Bloom's argument that there is a Western canon of common literature that all need to know is so out of fashion that his name does not exist in the mind of any new teacher. Not to worry, though; the education pendulum swings wide and broad, so before we know it, a back-to-basics movement will hit again. I figure I will see at least two more major changes before I retire.

Many theories work in controlled environments with small numbers, but pack a class with forty-plus students and see how well such novelties as "one-on-one portfolios" work. They were the *en vogue* method of assessment in the nineties. Watch one-hundred-pound teachers try to lug home thirty-pound boxes of portfolios. I have, and I've seen the destruction and emaciation. It may have seemed like a good idea on the university campus or in district office committee meetings, but when sixty-year-old Mrs. Smith throws her back out in the parking lot come December, it doesn't seem so good anymore.

One administrator suggested we discipline with watercolors, analyzing the student's subject matter and colors to ascertain the subconscious reason for defiance. He had, apparently, attended the same conference I did back when I taught middle school. A county program-development coordinator asserted, "There are no bad kids, just kids who do bad things," so suspending offending students should never be an option. A district science-restructuring program provided kits to middle school students so they could go all over campus and "do science." Students would explore the playground and blacktop like budding biologists looking for bacteria.

Each of these lunacies, based on the recommendations of a theorist's book, is a wonderful example of theory versus reality. Watercolors do not solve emotional or behavioral problems, but they do stain desks and tables. If students violently harass teachers and schoolmates day after day, would you not define them as bad? To the chagrin of curriculum coordinators, the science kits were destroyed within a week, and the students were running all over the place. The biologists turned into bacteria themselves, infecting the hallways with noise, the playground with trash, and the teacher with headaches.

In the end, the educational castle is a wonderful place to inhabit because it never gets invaded except by bad philosophy and theory. However, it is often a place of fairy-tale decisions that put teachers in situations as horrible as those of the unarmed Russian soldiers in World War II who stormed into battle against the Germans with the orders, "Follow the first soldier with the gun. When he gets killed, pick up his gun and keep going." Still, the pizza is tasty if you can sneak into the palace, and the coffee is always hot. If Duncan had been an administrator instead of a monarch, he probably would have written a dozen books and retired at fifty-five to a life of consulting.

In *Macbeth*, King Duncan is not a bawdy coxcomb in the style of Dogberry in *Much Ado about Nothing*; neither is he a prattling ass à la Bottom in *A Midsummer Night's Dream*, but he is a fool nevertheless. Gracious and harmless, overtrusting of his captain Macbeth and unaware of the witches' prophecies, Duncan is dispatched during the night in the title character's castle at Inverness, whose air he had described just that afternoon as "sweet" and "delicate." Though goodhearted and well intentioned, he falls prey to the disloyalty of his subordinate and to his romantic faith in wild, medieval Scotland's submission to royal succession.

In that Duncan's fatal flaw is his idealistic failure to develop an effective, reality-based intelligence network among his subjects, he is too often a blueprint for the educational administrators of today, a society that includes district superintendents, trustees, presidents, principals, headmasters, vice-principals, and in some locales, even deans or counselors. Many of these worthies are so far removed from the trenches that, like Duncan after the battle at Fife, they are condemned to their faith in romantic dreams about the modern battlefield of American education, when the reality lies in Macbeth's blood-and-guts familiarity with combat that parallels the atmosphere in today's classrooms, our contemporary trenches.

Were the hell to which this consigns many administrators merely their personal fate, it might be overlooked as wages deserved of their failure to pay attention. Regrettably, though, their inattention too frequently condemns their subjects—the students they're supposed to be educating—to lives misguided by insubstantial boundaries and false expectations. Sounds a bit like Duncan and his sons to me. Still, in the mode of Clint Eastwood's *The Good, the Bad and the Ugly*, there are many categories of administrators.

The *Macbeth* drama gives little more than a hint about King Duncan's successor, his son Malcolm. One can almost sympathize with Macbeth as he gets bloody "for God and country" during battle, only to have Duncan name Malcolm, who does nothing to deserve it, as next in line to rule. We can hypothesize that, once he eliminated Macbeth the usurper, Malcolm might have done no worse than his father. He lets those around him fight the battle as he climbs Dunsinane Hill to take the unguarded castle. After all, he and his brother feasted and drank along with their father in Inverness and then went straight to bed, so they couldn't have been much attuned to the machinations of the Macbeths.

Like Duncan, many administrators fall into the bad or naïve category. The word *bad* here is not used in a moral sense, as Duncan was squeaky clean in his doings, but in terms of performance and the application of reason and common sense. The *good* make positive contributions to the atmosphere and function of a school. The *bad*, at their very best, manage to have no impact at all, so the best of the bad are still in the top quartile of the administrative population. Members of this top *bad* segment adhere to the maxim, "Do no harm." The *ugly* can destroy a school in just a short time if allowed. They switch visions immediately, make draconian decisions, and ultimately make people "flee in all directions," similar to the way the reign of Macbeth affected the citizens of Scotland.

My Clint Eastwood *good* character, the principal of a K–8 school, showed his colors the day I was sent in after my initial interview with the district personnel director. He welcomed me into his Spartan office, had a twenty-minute conversation with me, and then invited me to return a fortnight later for a second interview with the entire faculty. This was unprecedented. Was this principal's faculty to be consulted prior to a hiring decision? What a great idea! After all, these would be my colleagues, and such an interview setting would enable me to probe day-to-day issues that affect teachers. I was impressed.

From the outset, I saw that the principal gave the faculty democratic decision-making authority in all matters that affected them as a group—details such as supervision scheduling, playground rules, faculty meeting frequency, and textbook selection. What was more, his default setting when issues arose with students or parents was to stand solidly behind the faculty. You can perhaps imagine the loyalty this engendered.

In one memorable case, a student who was a frequent disturbance and who had previously been suspended in school several times for the rest of day due to his misbehavior was again referred by his teacher. Clint Eastwood had had enough. When, as usual, both parents said the boy could not be sent home because they were at their places of employment, the principal loaded the miscreant into his car, drove him to the father's workplace, and delivered him to his dad's office. There was never another problem with that student.

A good administrator will probably cross a typical teacher's career path two or three times, but when you have one, you know it immediately and lament the day you lose such people. They are worth their weight in gold.

Some teachers become administrators with all the right intentions yet choose to go back to the classroom for one simple reason: bad teachers. A well-respected teacher on our campus moved to the vice-principal position, where his eyes were opened to the world of teachers who could not control their classes, handle their own curricula or bridle their own tongues. He could not support teachers when their disciplinary complaints about students were laughable.

This referral-writing mafia attempts to protect their classroom peace by tossing kids out right and left rather than find solutions to their own problems. Referrals for gum chewing, for eye rolling, for having a blue pen instead of a black one, and for talking out of turn become a blizzard of paperwork. Hours are spent disciplining students for mundane and minor offenses that any solid teacher can take care of on the spot with assertive discipline and a little know-how. When your neighbor says something rude, you do not call the police; when your neighbor's dog walks on your lawn, you do not call animal control; when you see a shooting star, you do not call NASA. Nevertheless, a handful of teachers on every campus are willing to start World War III instead of putting their feet across the metaphoric rule border.

A veteran teacher once told me, "The moment you become a referral writer, you lose all credibility with your students. You send the message that you cannot control your class, so you need someone else to do it." Many good administrators choose to survive by either heading back to the classroom to handle their own world or by running to higher ground off campus at the district office. I do not envy the good administrator who cares about education and works daily in the mud with the rest of us. I try to remember that when I'm tempted to write a referral, which I have not done in years.

14

THE PLOT LEADS TO A WINDOW

Welcome hither:
I have begun to plant thee, and will labour
To make thee full of growing.
Macbeth Act I

One of my Facebook contacts posted recently, "My life has a superb cast, but I don't know the plot."

One convenient way in which literature contrasts with reality is that we do get the whole plot in fairly short order. That's one reason literature appeals so much to our hearts, minds, and souls: we get the answers to its questions, at least within its confined borders.

However, the most ordinary real life being far more complex than the most convoluted fictional one, there will always be a disconnect between our own lives and those of the literary characters with whom we "interact." We can look to them for hypothetical scenarios, but we can never rely on them for guidance. Our lives become a "plot line" only in hindsight, when we've analyzed the twists and turns that brought us through our crises. As such, we experience a sequence of comedies and tragedies as we pass through the seven ages Jaques numbered in the Bard's *As You Like It*.

Of course, we also experience the vicissitudes of the lives of others such as family members, friends, and celebrities. For teachers, though, there's a whole gang of plot lines whose resolutions are lost in the fog of the unknown: those of our former students.

His agrarian society in Galilee understood well Jesus's parable of the sower, in which he talked about the different places seeds can fall when they're scattered by hand. We teachers "get" the application of this lesson to our profession, which is just as horticultural as that of a farmer, but with one big difference: farmers get to see the fruit of their efforts. Teachers rarely get to see much beyond a glimmer of the future gem at best, and it can be a Star of India sapphire or Blue Heart diamond moment (or, sadly, even a lump-of-coal moment) anytime we get to see the mature result of our work. Knight-errant farmers all, we teachers joust with the elements of our environment—people, buildings, clocks, and even weather—hoping that the speed of our charges and the power of our lance thrusts will plant deeply into fertile soil the seeds of knowledge and wisdom.

Like the sun whose rays the Lord makes to shine on the evil and the good, we sow our seeds on all students without regard for preexisting circumstances and hope for the best from every student. We believe in excellence. In fact, some superidealists such as myself even fancy that every child is gifted if only we can find the key to unlock his or her treasure chest. Still, even if we do discover that key, we rarely get more than a peek at the treasure.

In reflecting on forty years of teaching elementary, junior high, and high school, I can come up with only a handful of hints about how a given student seed matured. That's because education takes years, and we rarely maintain contact for that long. It's not like being an automotive mechanic, who sees the immediate result of the repairs he or she has made. Neither is it like construction work, where the new structure is a visible measure of achievement. It's not even like something as mundane as washing a mirror, where clarity gives a clear reflection and where streaks show the washer's flaws. Students move on from our campus to the next level, follow their families to new locations, drop out, or in some other way blip off our radar screens. And there are so many of them!

In my imagination, I envisage a grand reunion someday of all the students I have taught—there'd be thousands of them—just so I could hear their stories. Most I'd be delighted to see, some perhaps not so much, but just not knowing gnaws at me. Some have entered the very profession I dedicated my own life to. I am always happy and sad for them in a single moment, if that makes any sense. I know what awaits them in the classroom, and many—most, actually—were students with no idea how crazy things were around them, floating through school with rose-colored glasses on and skipping to class (metaphorically, of course). True idealists all, they get quite the shock in their first year of teaching.

One in particular majored in two romance tongues in college, during which she traveled about the world, exercising her linguistic and social skills; she was hired straight out of her BA program as an instructor in the modern languages program at her alma mater. I got a kick out of her reaction to her first week of teaching. The lesson for her first day vaporized when the classroom computer hadn't cooperated. She commented that she had been exhausted by Wednesday afternoon but still had to grade papers and plan lessons for the next two days before she could rest. Ah, yes, the transition from student to teacher is a chasm even Evel Knievel would have been wary of jumping.

Ever the teacher, I warned her never again to depend solely on technology and advised her to sanitize her online persona now that she was no longer a co-ed: some eighteen-year-old male student in her class might see his bikini-clad instructor on Facebook with come-hither eyes. With today's social media, students will Google teachers and instantly find embarrassing pictures if the instructor is not careful. At my school, we had an English teacher who students found out had been a former member of MTV's *Real World*. Some of her old exploits could still be found online through streaming video. In one episode, her comments about the male anatomy while doing tequila shots with other cast members made her an instant legend with our teen male population.

Recently, I was entertained by my former student's Facebook comment about how welcome fall break was so she could get some rest from teaching. I reminded her of how she and her classmates used to laugh when I told them that teachers were the happiest people of all on campus when vacations came along. I think she understands now. Many others don't make it beyond their first year.

I interviewed for a job once, following one of my former students who had interviewed just an hour before. The interview committee recognized my name because she had commented that she went into teaching because of a high school teacher and named me specifically. I told them to hire her before me because I already had a job. They hired us both. What a great compliment. She quit by May.

She said that the students "looked at her like they hated her" each day. I told her that it was just how teens look most of the time, but when she was a student in my class, she was always smiling and nodding at what I had to say. Poor kid. Teens look angry most of the time. They are not, though. And the looks rarely change except for those of seniors during the last week of school. I notice some very big, bright, and scared eyes in those final hours of high school bliss.

For seniors, that last day of high school is always bittersweet for me and for them. Their journey, now complete, places them in a strange moment in their lives where they settle briefly before heading out again into deep, difficult, stormy seas through which they have not yet navigated. My last bit of advice to students when they leave my class for college consists of the following:

> When you get to school, find a place in the library where no one can find you. Locate the dusty and profound location where you can have total quiet, perhaps among the stacks or hidden passageways. Use that special place to think, to read, and to reflect on your life

and the human condition. Make it your special spot, where the great thoughts and concerns of the centuries can run through your brain and engage with your own dreams and concerns. Let nothing deter you from getting to that spot several times a week before your life adds a job, taxes, a spouse, children, life insurance, mutual funds, retirement, and utility bills, not to mention dishes to rinse.

Last year, a former student e-mailed me from her "spot" at UC Santa Barbara. She found a certain desk near a window in the campus library and made that her place of study and reflection for four years. In her final semester, she thanked me for my suggestion. She said that her seat of transformation looked out on the Pacific, into which the tangerine sun shimmered away each evening. "Gorgeous fails to describe it!" she marveled. I figured if we'd been actually speaking to each other, she'd have said this in an awed whisper.

Her entire college experience was captured in that one moment, and she just had to tell me about it. As she pored over philosophy, literature, religion, history, science, and the world's greatest ideas, the window called to her each day. "Though I've changed," she commented, "this place never has." The sun retired each day through the same window, but somehow, she sat there different from the first-year student she had been. Nature, combined with words, sprinkled with thought and reflection—a Romantic vision indeed!

As teachers, we, too, sit before such windows each day, facing a sea of children waiting for us to notice their individual beauty. Sometimes it takes time to see that beauty. The light needs a new angle, the weather must change, the shadows conceal what is truly there, but make no mistake about it, there is beauty in each student. Make sure you look often enough, and at some point, the light will hit just right and you will see it. Our desks are our own special places, but we have to make sure to look up once in a while to spy what is special and not just to tell them to be quiet and toss out their gum.

What a blessing it is to have an entire career with such a view. We sit, worn and weathered idealists—Don Quixote types, if you will—staring out at the vista, but when that last sun slips away, like my former student, we will know we chose wisely. We, too, will have changed, but the window will remain, and the sea beyond it will be as gorgeous and as worthy of taking the time to admire as ever. Thus can we remain forever young.

Oh, and we most certainly will remember how to spell *McBeth*… uh…*Macbeth*.